■■■■■■■■■■■■■■■■■■■■■■

A BOWL
OF CHERRIES

■   ■

A BOWL
OF
CHERRIES

∎

SHENA
MACKAY

∎

MOYER BELL
Wakefield, Rhode Island & London

■ ■

Published by Moyer Bell
Copyright © 1992 by Shena Mackay

This book was originally published in Great Britain by The
Harvester Press Ltd. 1984.

First Paperback Edition

■ ■

LIBRARY OF CONGRESS
CATALOGING IN PUBLICATION DATA

Mackay, Shena
    A bowl of cherries / Shena Mackay.
    p. cm.
    ISBN 1-55921-114-8
    I. Title.

PR6063.A2425B69   1992   91-35070
823'.914—dc20   CIP

■ ■

Printed in the United States of America
Distributed in North America by Publishers Group West, P.O. Box
8843, Emeryville, CA 94662, 800-788-3123 (in California 510-658-
3453), and in Europe by Gazelle Book Services Ltd., Falcon House,
Queen Square, Lancaster LA1 1RN England, 524-68765.

■■■■■■■■■■■■■■■■■■■■■■

To Brigid

■   ■

■ CHAPTER ONE ■

The lush, green, horse-studded landscape was taken over by trees as he climbed. The road was now a narrow tunnel winding through rising sandy banks knotted with roots; it was as though the trees on either side had started once to march down to the road and their antlers had locked in combat. The pale urban boy, increasingly uneasy at the loss of light, tried to jog a little but the heavy army boots he wore were rubbing sore watery sacs along the backs of his heels and every painful step, it seemed, must burst them, glueing his socks to his feet. Raw khaki chafed his wrists and the insides of his legs and had raised a red semi-circle along his white neck. He had very white skin and his pale green eyes, like pebbles under water, flickered anxiously from side to side and over his shoulder at every crack of twig, rustle of bird or animal in the undergrowth. Two huge white eyes suddenly veered out at him. He flattened himself against the bank until he saw that they were the white ends of hewn tree trunks. He swore, the words hung like dirty smoke in the still air.

When he stepped out again, in control of his heart beats, there was a crashing, cracking of branches breaking, great ragged gasps; an enormous body plunged over him, a hoof clipped a burning line across his head, hooves cracked across the road and diminished in the sand and leaf falls on the opposite bank. The reek of sweat dissipated in the dampness.

His skull was falling apart; he sat in the road, holding the two halves together like a split apple. After some minutes, he removed one hand gingerly and ran a finger along the bloody parting in his hair; it seemed that his head was still intact. He lurched across the road and, grabbing roots, hauled himself up the bank and landed on his knees in a thicket of bilberry bushes and stood up to find himself in a little track beaten down by the horse. He examined the scratches on his hands, as one unaccustomed to such things, and climbed upwards through beech and birch and bracken; cold berries dangled against his face; now the ground changed into soft piles of pine-needles, invading his shoes, and the air was sour and fungoid. He was lost in a maze of pines. He blundered on, not knowing if he was awake or asleep in one of his dreams of wandering through strange landscapes; wide plains where pre-historic ruminants suddenly raised their heads from grazing to charge; or climbing endless intricate steel staircases, white-lit tunnels; fleeing through ornately furnished and brocaded rooms and tapestried corridors of empty mansions; sitting in dark trains and suddenly seeing the incomprehensible name of a wrong station flashing past.

'If I am asleep I will wake up,' he thought, 'or perhaps I am dead – killed by that horse, and the dreams were a presentiment of the hell in which I am doomed to wander endlessly.'

His head was aching badly and the next time he tripped he rolled under a tree which spread its branches to the ground like a dark umbrella, and eased himself into the soft bowl beneath and, with no thought of why he was there, fell asleep.

He was half-dreaming of a black sky with two moons. He opened his eyes; the moon hung high above the leaves. He crawled out; stars shimmered among clouds and a crescent-shaped light shone from the window of a black house in the valley below him. He could see now that he was at the edge of the wood and if he climbed a fence and crossed two sloping fields he could reach the house.

Great drenched cattle lay in the grass and lifted their heads but did not attack as he passed among them. He longed to release his feet from the torturing boots and feel the cold grass on them, but the laces were tied in sodden sandy knots and he feared lurking snakes and thistles. His trousers soaked up the dew until they were soggy to the knees. His body felt light and empty like a skeleton leaf bowled along by the wind. At last he climbed a low stone wall, fuzzy with plants and lichens, and stood in the gardens of the house called St Cloud. Black trees rustled, black water glittered. Whoever had ordered the boxy burglar alarm jutting from the wall had neglected to close the little scimitar-shaped upstairs window lit from within like a crescent moon. The thick stems of ancient creeper provided an easy ladder. He landed on soft carpet in the soft air of the sleeping house.

Snoring mowed the air, cut swathes through the darkness,

deadening the banging of his heart which, it seemed, must set the whole house jangling. His hands tightened into fists. A clock's chime flattened him against the wall between two heavy chests but the rhythm of the snores was unbroken. He tried a little door at the end of the passage; it opened onto a narrow flight of uncarpeted stairs. They shrieked under his boots and the door at the top screamed back at them as he opened it and closed it behind him, wedging a chairback under the handle, and stood in a shaft of pearly moonlight. Beads from a broken necklace rolled under his feet as he stepped forward, dusty pearls; oyster satin dancing shoes pointed their toes, frozen in a ghostly foxtrot; the amber eyes of a fox fur dangling over a chair back glittered sightlessly at handbags, boxes, a chipped bowl and ewer. A table under the window was cluttered with candlesticks, picture frames, photographs, tortoiseshell combs, clips, rhinestones, a butterfly wing cigarette case, magazines, a sea horse, artificial flowers, a champagne cork; dead ephemera glimmering in the moonlight's lustre. A baby's cot was folded against the wall. He ripped off the intolerable uniform and stood for a few moments letting the moonlight lap his sore skin like cool water. A long chest stood against a wall; flakes of old gold paint fell from his fingers as he lifted its lid. He threw out a pile of mothy army blankets and heaps of photographs and then he encountered a heavy manila envelope and drew out of it a sheaf of papers, half-charred and stained, as if they had been pulled from a fire and soused with water. He knelt down to read them, then, shivering, reached for something to wrap round himself. He pulled a once-white satin and tulle dress from a chair and, putting it round his shoulders, stared at the blotchy words like drowned crane flies in dry pools of ink.

He had read the words before, but not in this form. He had seen this long-legged writing before, but not saying these words. He put two of the blankets back in the chest and climbed in, wrapping himself in the satin dress to ward off itchiness, pulled the other blanket on top of him and soon fell asleep. The blanket slipped back from his shoulder and he lay in the moonlight, mouth slightly open, like a drunken bride in a coffin.

Downstairs, in the master bedroom, Rex's lips parted in a slight smile. He was swimming across a lake. The stems of lilies parted gently as he swam and closed slowly on the glassy green path he clove through the water, each flower incandescent, filled with light, opened to show golden filaments drenched with a sweet scent. He was aware of being perfectly happy. 'Praise my soul the King of Heaven' burst from his lips and the sound of a great orchestra swelled from the lilies and filled the air. He longed for the lake to be endless, suspended in eternity, so that he could swim like this forever through the music and the lilies, but on the bank stood his brother and then he was in his arms, weeping on his shoulder tears of pure joy. 'Ransomed, healed, restored, forgiven . . .'

He woke to immediate disappointment so bitter that a thick tear ran from each eye into the pillow in which he buried his face to hide from the morning which had snatched perfect happiness from him. He was lured out by the smell of coffee rising from a cup on the little table beside the bed. Music from a radio downstairs drifted through the floor. 'What'll I do with just a photograph to tell my troubles to?' Why were they playing that old song now that his father used to sing? Rex took a sip of his coffee and rose heavily and walked over to the looking-glass.

'Weltschmertz,' he said. 'Angst,' replied the tall blond tousled man in a striped nightshirt who stared back at him.

'What's it all for?', he asked as he poured oil from a cut-glass decanter into his bath and stepped into the blue foam. 'What'll I do when you are far away and I am blue, what'll I do?' he hummed. Why should anyone play that old song now, that Father used to sing when Father and Mother, both dead, and brother, dead to him, were so happy; at least Father, Mother and he had been so happy; he didn't know if Stanley had ever been so. 'I was good then,' he said aloud to the steam blooming round the gold taps. 'I could'a had class. I could'a bin a contender.'

'But I am a contender,' he cried, springing up girdled with bubbles. What if everything he had written for the last thirty years, however successful in terms of sales, had been compared un-favourably by the critics to *Silence*. Work, work, work; that was his only salvation. Back in the bedroom his sleeve caught the rim of the cup as he dressed. The coffee spread in a slow stain into the washed silk carpet.

'You might have brought your cup down,' complained Daphne, his wife, looking up from the newspaper. 'It really isn't fair on Mrs

Finch.' He sat down opposite her at the breakfast table, savage because she had got *The Times* first, and poured himself another cup of coffee.

'Oh! isn't that nice,' she cried. 'To Penny and James, twin daughters, (Lucy and Emily) sisters for Piers, Dominic, Toby, Edward and Christian. Deo Gratias.'

'I don't see anything nice in that. In very poor taste, advertising such incontinence, I should think.'

'They must be so happy. How they longed for a little girl to complete their family. And now they've got two – what a blessed bonus. I can just see the little boys, filing into the nursery, Piers, his little face all solemn and screwed up, very much the elder brother, has his finger on his lips as they peep into the twin white cradles bedecked with pink –'

'If I might be permitted to glance at the Deaths,' broke in Rex.

'I think I'll write a story about that little family,' Daphne went on. 'Only I think I might make the babies handicapped,' she added thoughtfully, staring into the marmalade as Rex snatched the paper from her. 'That's the difference between us – I read the Births first, you read the Deaths. I wonder whose death you hope to see anyway? I admit to being snobbish enough to assume that anyone I know would be in the obituaries. Well, I'll leave you to it, you old ghoul.' She pecked dryly at his forehead. 'See you at elevenses. Thank God I'm on the side of Life!' she flung back at him.

'I notice neither of us reads the marriages,' he muttered as he found she had eaten all the toast. He picked up a spoon and was caught eating marmalade from the jar by Mrs Finch when she made her silent entrance.

Upstairs in the attic a boy was wrestling with the two problems of the bathroom and breakfast. As Mrs Finch stood at the kitchen sink she thought she saw a figure dodge behind a tree in the garden but when she opened the back door she could see no one.

At eleven o'clock she carried a silver tray of coffee and biscuits into the morning room and rang a little bell to summon Rex and Daphne from their respective rooms. They almost scampered in like children released from lessons, tall, elegant children freed from spilling words out of their coiffured heads.

'Ah, coffee. Nothing like it for restoring the old parched grey matter!' said Lord Muck, rubbing his hands as he did every morning.

'Choccy biccies! Mrs Finch, you spoil us!' said Lady Muck, taking two, as if she hadn't written chocolate biscuits herself on the shopping list she left for Mrs Finch on a melamine board on the kitchen wall, so that Mrs Finch had to copy it down on a piece of paper.

'Get much work done?' asked Daphne.

'I've given the kitchen a thorough going-over and done the stairs and the bedrooms. I managed to get that stain out of the Chinese carpet. I took a J-cloth and a bit of . . .'

'Dear Finchy, I'm sure you've done lots of marvellous things. I don't know how we'd manage without you, but I was actually speaking to Rex. . . .'

'Pardon me, I'm sure,' said Mrs Finch and left the room.

'As a matter of fact I haven't.' Rex had stood by the window watching the clouds drift across the lake. St Cloud, which he had inherited from his father, took its name, he had imagined as a child, from the clouds mirrored in the lilies and rushes of its small lake. His father had stipulated that the grey house, hung with green creepers that burned scarlet in autumn so that it seemed that flames ran up the walls, go to his elder son; in fact his second son Stanley was only five minutes younger than Rex.

He had been standing watching the clouds when the telephone rang.

'Maud rang. It seems that Seamus has disappeared.'

Daphne fitted a black Sobranie into a black and marcasite holder and waited for Rex to light it.

'What a bore,' said Rex, voicing their joint verdict. 'What does she expect me to do about it?' They both knew he would do nothing.

'When she insisted on calling him Seamus I didn't realise he would take it literally.'

Seamus was the result of an affair he had had some fifteen years ago, now much regretted. Daphne never forgot to send a birthday card to Seamus; some of them still withered dustily, unopened, on hall tables in various rooming houses in North London. She had once intercepted an ill-spelled request for football boots and had purchased a pair two sizes too large to allow for growth and with plastic studs instead of the metal ones he had stipulated, for she assumed that Seamus was an unsporting little boy who would kick his opponents, and posted them off. There had been no acknowledgment. Nor had there been any thanks for Rex's old copies of *Bevis, the Story of a Boy* and *Stalky & Co.* Daphne every year also wrote his birthday in large black letters on Rex's engagement calendar lest he forget either his sin or her forgiveness of it.

'I told you it would be unkind to take him away from that council school,' she said now. 'It was obvious to me that the poor child would be a fish out of water among nicely brought-up boys.'

▪ CHAPTER TWO ▪

Three red-brick villas, Faith, Hope and Charity, stood together in a back street in Dorking. Stanley Beaumont leaned against the window of an upstairs room in Hope Villa, as inappropriately named a domicile for him as either of its neighbours, a caricature or cheap copy of his brother Rex. Whereas Rex's legs were long and slim, Stanley's were thin and slightly bowed; Rex's hair was still a golden crown, and his brother's dry brown curls were tipped with grey; large blue eyes looked out of both faces but Stanley's were a paler blue and blinked behind a pair of glasses which at some time had required first-aid with elastoplast. Rex's body, lissom from regular games of squash, was clothed in soft silks and cashmeres; Stanley's corduroy trousers had come from Tesco and his yellowed linen jacket and shirt were from the Help the Aged shop and still bore a faint sour smell from rubbing shoulders with the clothes of the dead. A white coat, blotched with tomato sauce, and a pair of checked cook's trousers hung on the back of the door. It was always raining outside Stanley's window; a dripping overflow which he had failed to fix and no one else had bothered to, splashed down relentlessly. He had let his watch get into the steam of the kettle; its face was blurred like an old servant in tears, and foolish tears started into his own eyes at the sight of a young mother with a pram in the sun. Bright chrome wheels rolled, the baby laughed, birds sang, bees flew in and out of the purple irises whose green blades stabbed his heart; all getting on with their lives, all with a purpose. He turned away from the window, wiping the mist from his glasses. To face, each morning, at his age, this brown carpet, this chipped veneer chest of drawers, to scrape the face staring out of a speckled glass balanced above the sink behind a curtain hung on a rusty string, to heat little messes of food on a Baby Belling in the corner of a rented room, and use a shared bathroom surreptitiously; to know that his body has proved worthy of this stained moquette chair and that at the end of the day it must subside into this narrow, lumpy bed, to know all this and to rise again each morning demands a sort of heroism.

The overflow dripped; reedy music wailed from the radio. Stanley, anticipating the high spot of his day, assembled the constituents of happiness: the *Times* crossword, a sharp pencil, a packet containing two cigarettes, a book of matches bearing the name La Golondrina. Downstairs the clock struck nine. Transitory pleasure. At nine-fifteen he was faced with that deadest of artifacts, a completed crossword puzzle. Before ten o'clock he had composed an alternative set of clues. He smoked his second cigarette. He read the paper; births, deaths, marriages, wars, sport, business, courtrooms; all in another world from his little cell. He made some Camp coffee and washed his cup and saucer. He washed a shirt and pair of pants and socks and hung them on a string across the window to dry. At last, there being nothing else to do, he reeled a piece of paper into his old black typewriter.

'I'm here.'

He typed a swear word without looking up and then a row of xxxs over it.

'Me's come,' the voice amended, perhaps thinking that a cuter statement would elicit a response.

'So I see.'

The little figure of his landlady's three-year-old grandson Jason, who lived with her, his mother being absent more often than not and his father unknown, stood in the doorway, thumbs stuck in the straps of his dungarees, the sun making a golden aureole of his curly head.

'Wotcher doin'?' said Jason, coming in and putting a tiny grimy hand on the typewriter. Stanley wondered, as often before, how he could be so dirty so early in the morning.

'Incha got nothin' to do?' he asked kindly.

'Yes.'

'Can I have a drink?'

'No.'

'I'm firsty.' The soft lips trembled threateningly.

'I haven't got anything you like – only coffee.'

'I like coffee.' Jason jumped heavily up and down in a display of enthusiasm.

In a second Stanley saw himself rising, making a cup of coffee and handing it to Jason who gulped it, scalded his mouth, howled and dropped the cup, scalding his chest. Ambulance, accusations, remorse, remorse.

'I'm going to get my bottle and you can put some coffee in it for me.'

Stanley recalled having seen a baby's bottle of greyish brown liquid suspended from Jason's mouth.

'No,' he roared.

Jason opened his mouth and emitted a prolonged wail which gradually trailed away round the bend of the stairs.

Stanley heard a woman's voice shout, 'I've had just about enough of you! Get to bed!'

After this Stanley couldn't settle to his typing; Jason's misery oozed like heavy vapour through the floorboards. He took his shopping bag and set out for the shops. Involuntarily he glanced up as he closed the gate and saw a little face, thumb in mouth, finger in nose, resting against a fluffy animal at an upstairs window. As he closed the gate, the front door opened and his landlady, head bristling with rollers under a chiffon scarf shouted, 'You're wanted on the phone!'

'Me? Who? Why? Thank you,' gasped Stanley all at once as he fumbled with the gate and barged clumsily back in with his shopping bag, tripping over a hoover. In all the years he had lived in this house he had never had a phone call.

'I hope you're not going to make a habit of this,' said Mr. Herring, standing in the doorway of her lounge to witness this unprecedented occurrence. As Stanley picked up the telephone anxiety suffused his chest so that he could hardly croak 'Hello.' A strong cosmetic scent came from the receiver.

'Stanley Beaumont?'

'This is Martin Timothy.' He paused as if expecting a reaction but when only the sound of a hoover came from his earpiece, went on '. . . I've had an awful job tracking you down. No one seemed to know where to get hold of you.'

He might as well have added, 'Everybody, if they had heard of you, assumed that you were dead.'

'Then I hit on the idea of contacting your brother. I'm sorry, did you say something? Anyway—I've just taken over the poetry list at Wimbush and Plant. I'm compiling a new anthology of Second World War poets and I thought it would be nice to include some pieces by conscientious objectors, to give the other side of the picture, as it were; I wondered if we could have lunch? How about Tuesday next week, do you know Feely's? Good. One o'clock on Tuesday then. I look forward to it.'

Click. Stanley was left standing with the dialling tone boring into his ear.

'I hope this isn't the thin edge of the wedge,' said Mrs Herring in a voice full of dust.

'The other side of the picture,' said Stanley in his room.

He saw as if in an old film Rex and Daphne at the altar, Daphne in a white dress, Rex's arm distinguished by a sling. Behind them, in the front pew, his parents, Ronnie and Boy. Ronnie bidding to outshine the bride and Major 'Boy' Beaumont in dress uniform. His own nails, still grained with coaldust on the prayer book, a bubble in his throat blocking the cry that it was he who should be standing there with Daphne, that Rex had stolen his girl. The reception, and Ronnie plucking a white feather from her boa and handing it to him in front of all the guests; her disgraced son who was a conchie and had been sent from prison down the mine. Ronnie and Boy had been killed when a palm tree crashed onto their car on the Corniche and Stanley was left unabsolved.

It seemed that since then he had dedicated his life to becoming the poor specimen they had thought him, as if he might redeem himself by proving them right. When Ronnie had read the story of the Sleeping Beauty to her twins, Rex's golden head nestling in her lap and Stanley coffined in his sheets, fingering his eczema, it seemed to him that at their christening the good fairy hadn't known there were two babies and had given all her gifts to Rex and then the bad fairy had flown in and pointed at Stanley and screeched, 'He shall have glasses and eczema and keep falling over and nobody will care when he hurts his knees.' His father came into the nursery.

'All aboard the Dreamland Express!'

He hooted like a train and put his hands round Ronnie's waist and they chugged out of the room.

Stanley had sent Ronnie and Boy a copy of his book of poems entitled *The Profane Comedy*, a set of cantos based on his experience in the pit; it came back by return post with two pages still uncut. Rex, healing his father's disappointment that he had not made the Army his career, brought glory to the family name with a novel which was said to speak for wartime youth. Rex and Daphne inherited St Cloud and embarked on their famous series of detective stories; they would sit at opposite ends of a polished table which reflected their silver inkstands, writing with feather pens, with bright young faces as their quills tore into the piles of white paper. A baby's crying disturbed their work and a young woman named Finch was brought in to quieten it.

The telephone call from Martin Timothy, absurd youth with two Christian names, had come several years too late. Stanley was like a prisoner who after years of trying to claw his way out of a dungeon has resigned himself to the darkness and crouches in a corner, hiding his eyes from the light when the cell door is at last opened. He had no intention of presenting his grey face at Feely's, whatever or wherever that was. How right Ronnie and Boy had been in returning 'The Profane Comedy' unread. He wished he had not read it himself. Even after all these years its memory brought a blush to his cheek. He cursed the publisher's lack of judgement, and cruelty in pandering to a young man's vanity. If he had not been taken in by those worthless vainglorious verses, Stanley might have been a happy man today instead of his brother's distorted shadow. He might have a wife and children, a little shop. He saw himself dipping a metal scoop into a bag of grain, harvests running through his fingers, gardens flowering in his hand. He might close the shop at night, pleasantly tired from a useful day's work and, over supper, amuse his wife with funny anecdotes about the customers. They would work in the garden together on Sundays and take the dog for walks and visit their grandchildren, for the children would be grown-up by now and they could look back and laugh over the worries and sleepless nights spent over measles and exams, and unsuitable boyfriends. A son might even join him in the business, and they might expand and take over the premises next door. A signpainter in white overalls put the finishing touch to the sign 'Stanley Beaumont and Son'. The family stood on the pavement looking up with pride. His wife's eyes were misty. Stanley knew what she was feeling and put his arm around her shoulder, giving it a little squeeze. His own eyes were not guiltless of moisture; he pretended he had got a fly in one of them, but she saw through him. She always did.

'You bloody old fool,' said Stanley aloud.

He stared angrily round his room. Why on earth had he thought he wanted that pink soapstone elephant, bought for a few pence at a jumble sale? Hadn't he known how it would stand on the dusty shelf trumpeting loneliness through its pink trunk?

▪ CHAPTER THREE ▪

Four months earlier Seamus and his mother had emerged from the
darkness of Archway Road tube station into sunshine splintered by
pneumatic drills and the sound of breaking pavements; the only
flowers here blossomed on the canopies of high glittering prams.
They walked for some time before turning into a side street,
checking house and shop numbers as they went until they stopped
between a small handbag factory and a Cypriot grocer's. Maud
rooted in the canvas sack she carried for a piece of paper.
Crouching down while lipsticks, cigarettes, books, papers, a comb,
an old orange, blue-green with mould, more poisonous puffball or
mossy tennis ball than fruit, flowed onto the pavement beside her.

'I think this orange is past its best. Put it in a litter bin, would you,
Seamus?' As he kicked it into the gutter, a greenish powder rose
from its skin.

'Ah! here it is. Yes, this is definitely the place but I can't think
that . . .'

It was a tall peeling grey-painted stucco building with the name
'Magic Carnival Novelties' in faded fairground lettering on a painted
sign above its door. Behind its dusty window lay heaps of glittering
excelsior, red, green, gold, blue, silver foil trumpets, feathered
squeakers, paper fans, black eye-masks and animal faces, a skull,
peashooters, magic daggers, tricks, jokes, little silk Chinese drums,
paper accordions, flutes, indoor fireworks, joss-sticks, balloons,
spangles, sparklers, sequins; gimcrack geegaws, evanescent
glitter.

A father, a mother and a child stopped beside Maud and Seamus
for a moment.

'Look at that! Oh, I wish I could have one of those!'

The parents on the hot pavement in the diesel fumes saw with
jaded adult eyes that the mouths of the trumpets were dimmed with
dust and their gold paint was cracking and the skins of the balloons
were wrinkling and perishing in the sun.

'You don't want none of those – they're a waste of money,' said the father, pulling the child along. 'Load of rubbish,' said the mother. 'Well, no use standing here melting in the sun,' said Maud and pushed open the shop door.

It seemed appropriate that the proprietor of this emporium should be a giant, the false nose he wore barely covered his own. When they entered he was demonstrating a set of fragile windchimes to a potential customer; the glass splintered at his breath. He picked up a paper fan which tore in his huge fingers and let it fall in a melancholy way to the floor; he shuffled through bits of broken toys as he escorted her to the door when she left without buying anything. His wares seemed designed to make any party a disaster. 'Good morning, Madam – may I help you?' he asked, turning to Maud. Her head just reached the expanding steel armbands he wore on his shirt-sleeves. Maud started to explain about the advertisement for accommodation when a bold balloon bobbed across the floor perilously near his feet. He stepped back on it. 'Ah! yes,' he said, ignoring the small explosion. 'If you would care to look at the rooms.' He led them up a broken wooden staircase to the top of the house; through open doors they could see stacks of old gilded picture frames, dusty stone figures of cherubs and nymphs, dry fountains, broken marble-topped tables, a tail-less rocking horse who stared at them with amber glass eyes.

'Would you look at the darling Dobbin,' cried Maud.

Seamus, who had been looking, averted his eyes. On the third floor the giant stopped in front of a closed door and turned the handle; it came off in his hand. He stuffed it in his pocket.

'Oh! dear.' He rattled hopelessly at the door.

'Never mind – we'll take the rooms,' said Maud.

'Of what does the accommodation consist?' she enquired in their new landlord's kitchen, where they had adjourned to talk terms.

'Two rooms, cooking facs, share bath,' he replied, pouring tea from a black pot which had a green rubber spout like that on the dripping tap. 'Your poor finger!' cried Maud, spotting a bloody bandage pierced by a nail. 'It's nothing – just a bit of fun,' he said, pulling it off to reveal a perfectly sound finger.

'Yours must be a very interesting business,' she said, paling.

'As businesses go,' he answered, taking a lump of sugar from the bowl and dropping it in his tea – 'as businesses go it's not what you'd call a going concern. As for being interesting, I suppose if I was more interested I'd be concerned about it not being a going concern. Or if I was busier I'd be less concerned and more interested.'

The sugar lump in his tea dissolved and a black plastic fly floated to the surface. He drank it. Seamus laughed.

'Seamus!' said his mother in a shocked tone.

'I see the boy's got a sense of humour – well, this is just the place for him. Dead flies?' He pulled packets of them from his pocket. 'Fool your friends, eh? Trick spider? Drop this one in your mother's tea – always good for a laugh. Rubber pencil – looks real doesn't it? Fool the teacher. Go on – try it!'

He handed Seamus the pencil and a scrap of paper. Seamus scribbled on it. 'It is real.'

'Fooled you, didn't I?' cried the giant.

'Excuse my asking,' said Maud, 'but you have a wonderful way with words. You haven't a bit of the Irish in you by any chance? I'm Irish myself.'

'I'm by way of being a bit of a poet,' said Seamus quietly, in imitation, expecting her to continue as she always did, but Maud had stopped speaking and only his voice was heard.

'A bit of a poet, are you lad? Well, I could tell that you were Irish. The boy has the features of a Paddy and the red hair!'

'My hair was twice the colour at his age,' said Maud, nettled, but Seamus looked as if he had been stung, red running up his neck fusing his freckles to the roots of his tight red curls.

'They say suffering takes the colour from your hair.' She patted hers which, by nature or henna, although darker than Seamus's, was still bright enough and lay in flat coppery tendrils on her shoulders. Seamus wondered how long it would take before she added their landlord to her circle of slaves.

'You must have a great time fooling your friends,' she said.

'I have no friends.'

'You've two friends now,' cried Maud. 'Hasn't he, Seamus?'

'Has he? Who?'

'Us, you fool!'

'Oh!'

'Excuse me – I think I hear that rarest of sounds, the ringing of the shop bell. You must show me some of your poetry sometime; only if you'd like to, of course,' he said to Seamus as he stood up.

'It's me that's the poet,' called Maud. 'I'm Maud Mandrake' – but he had gone. Seamus doubted if, anyway, he would have seen any of the slim pamphlets in which his mother's work appeared.

Later that day they moved in. A friend of Maud's brought their belongings round in a small van, then he and Maud set out to investigate her new local and Seamus was left to unpack. All day the sun had filtered through the grey lace curtains at the black window and baked the walls and spars of linoleum on the floor, which was neatly patched in places with squares of tin. A small sink with a rubber-spouted tap stood in a corner and there was a large wooden bedstead with steel springs but no mattress. The smaller room was seven feet square and held a camp bed and a paraffin stove.

Maud became full of energy. She got a job with a firm of jewellery repairers in Hatton Garden and sat all day at a bench threading tiny beads and seed pearls and cultured pearls and river pearls like babies' teeth under a dim bulb. The job was poorly paid but sufficed to pay the low rent. Seamus was enrolled at the local comprehensive. After work Maud would change into a pair of old trousers and scrub and paint and rip up the old splintered linoleum and lay new floor covering. She bought remnants in the market and cobbled two pairs of curtains and filled bottles and jars with flowers. She held a housewarming party; Seamus staggered home under a mountain of silver foil dishes from the Indian restaurant. He had declined to invite anyone.

'Never mind,' said Maud, 'you shall have a party for your own friends next month on your birthday.'

'My birthday was last month,' he pointed out.

'That's what I meant, you silly – a belated birthday party.'

Their landlord, Geoffrey Cruikshank as they learned his name to be, turned down Maud's invitation. His door was always shut. He had three records which he played regularly on his wind-up gramophone. In the morning while he dressed Maud and Seamus breakfasted to the strains of 'The Sun has got his Hat On'. Between one o'clock and two when the shop was closed for lunch, Seamus, if he happened to be playing truant, would turn up the volume of the television to drown 'Happy Days are Here Again' which after the twelfth hearing seemed to him to embrace all the sorrows of suffering humanity, and in the evening they imagined him capering heavily about his room in a toy helmet to the tune of 'The Laughing Policeman'. Despite the music, Seamus was very happy. Then, unfortunately, a string of pearls was found in Maud's handbag and things began to go wrong, as they always did.

*   *   *

Rex let the Bentley slide slowly down the street, past peeling terraces, a grubby launderette where a dusky housewife some nineteen years old sat knitting on the step, past shops whose bright foreign fruit and vegetables spilled out into wooden boxes on the pavement; past a chemist whose coloured waters had curdled in great dusty glass jars, and a handbag factory, past Magic Carnival Novelties. He drove on slowly towards a group of boys playing football. He braked and wound down the window. The boys stopped their game and stood in a tight bunch.

'I seem to have lost my way,' he started to say.

One of them disengaged his orange head from his companion's dark one and uttered some harsh adolescent cry and the others laughed raucously. Rex reversed rapidly, mounting the pavement and speeding away. His hands in their thin leather gloves were sweating on the wheel.

'My son,' he said aloud, bitterly.

When at last he arrived upstairs, directed there by a giant, he was sweating and bad-tempered.

'Oh! it's you,' said Maud, as if she had not summoned him on Toyland Post paper filched from the shop below.

'Weren't you expecting me? Is someone here?' he asked, looking round suspiciously.

'Seamus is out,' she answered coldly.

'I think I met him. He was very rude to me.'

'Why should he have been? He doesn't know you from Adam. Does Daphne know you've come?'

'Of course not.'

'Didn't she see the letter then?'

'I told her it was from a juvenile fan who had watched me on "The Book Programme".' He didn't want to confess how Daphne had prised it from his fingers.

'Ageing juvenile delinquent ex-fan,' she had said, tearing it up.

Rex had had to retrieve it from the dustbin under Mrs Finch's scornful eye and piece it together to find the address.

'Might I sit down?'

'Suit yourself,' shouted Maud; she had never bothered to be nice to Rex, over the sound of a pneumatic drill in the road outside.

'I was just going to have a coffee. Want some?'

'I would prefer an ice-cold drink if you've got one.'

'No fridge. There's some coke if you want it.'

He looked at the half-empty bottle standing in the sun beside a bottle of curdling milk. 'Coffee please.'

'Good Lord!' he remarked. 'I didn't know you could still get Camp coffee.'

'There are a lot of things you don't know. I don't suppose you know much about Social Security and Truant Officers either. Despite being such a famous chronicler of the contemporary scene. You'll have to have it black, the milk's gone off. How's whatsisname, your brother, Stanley, your twin?'

'You know I see as little of him as possible.'

'I think that's sad. Terribly sad when two brothers fall out.'

'We haven't fallen out. It's just that, as you know, we have so little in common.'

'It must be so embarrassing having him living in penury on your doorstep and you dining off the fat of the land in the great house that might have been his. Is there not a wing of the house or dower house or gamekeeper's cottage you could let him have?'

'My brother is not my keeper. Tell me about yourself, Maud – what have you been doing?' he said, making for safer ground but which might turn out to be a swamp.

'I could tell you that I've been doing a series of poetry readings in pubs, and the Arts Council are after me to do a tour, but it's not myself I want to talk about – it's Seamus. He needs a man's hand now; he's growing up. I was thinking – perhaps you would like to have him for a bit. Fair's fair, Rex, but I've had the bringing up of him for fourteen years and it wouldn't look good now, would it, if the Sunday papers or some posthumous biographer was to let the cat out of the bag that Rex Beaumont denied his own son and left him in penury without even a decent education while he was living off the fat of the land speaking at literary lunches and appearing on chat shows and quiz shows and God knows what?

'Do they never turn off that blasted pneumatic drill?' asked Rex pettishly. 'I thought British workmen were supposed to spend all their time leaning on their shovels – pity this lot don't!'

'They're Irish workmen,' cried Maud. 'Got you there!'

Rex had a vision of a sulky red-haired adolescent breaking china, lounging with his boots on the polished table while pop music blared out of the windows, smoking pot, sniffing glue, plunging a dirty syringe into a freckled arm, putting a match to St Cloud. Sweat was running down his chest and gathering in a pool at his belt.

'Don't let's quarrel, Maud. Yet, anyway,' he muttered to himself. 'We used to have glorious rows, didn't we?' he added wistfully.

'Don't bother to crinkle your eyes at me. The Rex Beaumont charm has lost its charm.' Rex's hand shook as he reached for his cup, spilling the coffee.

'I'll do it.' He jumped up. 'Where's the kitchen paper?'

'The what?'

'J-cloth then – anything – this stuff's dripping on my trousers!'

She threw a greyish cloth at him. It landed on the table like a heap of knitted porridge. Rex put his arm round her waist and pulled her to him.

'Get off! Do you think you can come here with your fancy talk of kitchen paper and J-cloths and take up where you left off fourteen years ago?'

'It was worth a try anyway.' He sat down again. At the most, he calculated, Seamus would have four more years at school – probably only two.

'I don't think it would be fair to ask Daphne to have Seamus to live with us, much as I'd like to. You know, Maud, it's been hard for me too, knowing that Seamus was growing up without me. I've missed the boy, Maud.'

Maud snorted.

'Don't think I don't feel guilty. I feel as guilty as hell! I only wish I could have done more.'

'You could have.'

'I'll tell you what. I'm willing to pay for Seamus to go to a decent school. A boarding school where they'll give him a sound education and knock the rough edges off him. Not that you haven't done a wonderful job, Maud, I'm sure of that,' he added hastily. 'Do stop chewing your nail polish, it can't taste nice and I'm sure it isn't good for you. It's probably what's best for the boy, Maud.'

'Since when did you worry about what's best for him? Or good for me? Actually, this nail varnish tastes very nice. Want a bite?' She poked a chipped red claw at his face.

'No, thank you.' He backed away. 'Anyway, Maud, think about it. I'll make some enquiries about schools and let you know.'

'Why wouldn't it be fair on Daphne?'

'She has her work. She's working flat out on a collection of short stories and she's half-way through a children's book that's way overdue.'

'Children's book! How ironic. What does she know about children?'

'She did bring up Daisy, you know, and we do have a granddaughter.'

'That Mrs Finch of yours brought Daisy up from what I've heard. Daphne was never a mother to her. When you two were off gallivanting all over the Continent, Daisy had to sleep in the pigsty with a pig. She told me.'

'Why are you trying to make me lose my temper? I won't lose it! Daisy did stay sometimes with Mrs Finch. Mrs Finch did keep a pig, I believe, but Daisy shared a room with Mrs Finch, certainly not with the pig! It was a small cottage.'

'Oh well, I expect Daisy got them confused. Mrs Finch used to put her nightdress on over her clothes when she went to bed. The pig's name was Baconbonce,' she concluded triumphantly.

'I'd no idea you and my daughter were such intimates.'

'Oh! we're not, we're not. I read her diary once. That time I came to St Cloud when Daphne was away. A terrible document reeking of loneliness, the pages glued together with tears, still damp to the touch. No, I don't suppose poor Daisy is intimate with anyone – let alone her stick of a husband. She's such a poor brainwashed colourless thing. Like a struck match.'

She lit a cigarette and held up the match. 'See? Only the head's burnt out and there's all that white virgin wood going to waste. The only time she showed a spark of life was when she ran off with that schoolmaster, and then you dragged her back – you and Daphne.' She flicked Daisy into an ash tray. She lay between them on the table.

'I'd better go. That is, if my car's still in one piece.'

'And what about my work? When I think of what I might have accomplished if I hadn't had your son hanging like a millstone round my neck! But you've never had any regard for my work have you?'

As Rex started the car which had, miraculously, not been vandalised, Maud's slatternly curves made a soft, regretted contrast to Daphne's elegant bones.

When he had gone, Maud was left picking bitterly at the grey string cloth, reflecting how her plan had gone wrong. She had convinced herself that Rex would take the boy, had even cried a little as she pictured the two of them rolling off in the car together, herself a lonely figure at the window; had even sent Seamus with all his clothes, except those he wore, in a bag to the launderette in readiness – and now Rex had gone without even giving her any money. She was left virtually penniless and with the prospect of telling Seamus that he was to be sent away to school.

'Cheapskate,' she said aloud, tearing the cloth. Where was Seamus? Gone off somewhere, she supposed. The selfishness of youth. She had promised herself that she wouldn't drink in the mornings, but half a teacup of vodka seemed to be justified. An hour later she was picking her way through derelicts sleeping in the sun in Soho Square, as she had swished through nettles and midges in Sligo many a year and bottle ago. John McArron was already at the bar of the dim pub, reflected in the mirror on the back wall among the jewelled bottles. He had arrived in London but six months ago with the manuscripts of two novels in his rucksack and already sycophants swam towards him affixing themselves like barnacles and whelks in the greenish light, and Maud, a shark in white cheesecloth, basked in his reflected glory. Now she feared that he was tiring of her; and she had to admit to herself that the Arts Council Tour was a timid promise, made under duress.

'A joke in a joke shop – that's what I've become.'

'It's because of John McArron you're sending me away. If I wasn't here he would move in with you.'

There he had hit the nail on the head! She could have hit him on the head, its red back towards her, bent over the ironing.

'Now darling, you know that's not true.'

'I won't go. You can't make me.'

The iron nosed expertly round a row of buttons. He didn't look up.

'I'm too old to go to school. Why can't I just leave school? I could leave school and just go off somewhere. Hitch-hike.'

'Now you're just being childish.'

'What about my friends then?'

'You'll make new friends. Nice boys who play musical instruments and speak Latin. You could learn the guitar or clarinet. You'd like that, wouldn't you?'

'I don't want to go to a boys' school.'

'Well, you can hardly go to a girls' school, now can you? Besides, you'll be home in the holidays – you can see your old friends then.

You never know, you might pal up with some nice boy who'll invite you home to his estate to stay; to meet his people.'

'And I'd invite him back here. I'm sure he would enjoy that.'

Maud sighed. 'Oh! you're impossible! Impossible and ungrateful. How did I come to have such a child?'

Answer came there none, except the hiss of a tear on hot iron. Seamus folded the dress and put it over the back of a chair. A fresh smell of wind-dried hot cotton filled the room. Maud became conscious of hunger. 'Is there anything to eat?'

'I got some chips earlier; I ate yours. I didn't think you'd be back tonight.'

'Never mind.'

'Don't I go out when you want me to? Didn't I make John McArron's breakfast when he stayed? Don't I shop and cook and clean and work my fingers to the bone to keep the home nice for you? Whose paper-round paid for the chips anyway?'

'It's true, Seamus, you do all those things. It's at no small sacrifice to myself that I'm sending you away.'

'Don't then.'

Maud looked thoughtful, staring at the pile of ironing as if she might read an answer there, then she said, 'That petticoat could do with a bit of a starch, I don't suppose—'

'Starch! Starch! You should have done what my father wanted you to do before I was born,' he muttered.

'What do you mean, Seamus?'

She was walking up Harley Street in her worn heels, the green leather peeling back over the white plastic cones beneath, that clopped with a hollow sound on the pavement. The brass plate and platinum-haired receptionist.

'You spent the money he gave you to get rid of me on a dress.'

'Who told you that?'

'You did.'

'Oh!' she said – a flat, long-drawn-out sound that seemed to acknowledge all her misfortunes, all her mistakes. It started to rain; a heavy rain that hit the lower window pane and turned it to a garden of silver lupins. Maud and Seamus seemed, in their hot box above the city traffic, in the night sky, suspended in time. If it could go on for ever, Seamus thought. The two of us here – me doing the ironing, an endless pile of frills and checks and cottons. Maud half rose from her chair to put her arm around him and say of course he needn't go; as if she would send her own boy away when she loved him more than anything or anyone in the world; but if she relaxed her hold someone else would get her teeth into John McArron and she would be lost. Sons were forever; she and Seamus would laugh together at this some day when he was grown up.

'You've changed your mind! I saw it in your face! I knew you wouldn't make me go,' cried Seamus, banging down the iron and falling on his knees beside her chair, wreathing his arms round her neck. Her hand strayed across his head, then suddenly she seized a red curl and pulled it hard.

'Has it never occurred to you that having a great teenage son hanging round can cast rather a blight on things?'

The blight left, a new boy in mid-term, with a suitcase full of new clothes. Geoffrey Cruikshank took him to Victoria Station in a cab. He bought him a bar of chocolate from a machine. His name, printed in biro, disappeared the first time anything was washed. Matron, in her white shoes, lay in wait for him in the corridors and asked, 'Hasn't your mother sent those name-tapes yet?'

▪ CHAPTER FOUR ▪

Daisy weighed in for the day at eight and a half stone. She sighed as she stepped from the scales. Her eyes flickered past her reflection in the blurry mirror. They were half-closed; had they been opened they would have been seen to be a light-blue but there was not often anything worth looking at to make them open wider. If Rex was gold and Daphne such dark metal, what could she be but some sort of alloy? She had failed to achieve bronze; her hair was what was called light-brown. She lay lapped by pearly bubbles in the bathroom of Fairlawn as the sound of the church clock struck seven through the steam. There was a rattling at the door.

'I just want to check that grouting,' came her husband's voice.

'Oh Julian – I'm in the bath.'

'It won't take a sec.'

She climbed out of the bath and put on a towelling robe and opened the door.

'How many times have I told you to open the window when you have a bath? Look at the condensation! Just as I thought,' he grumbled, poking at the tiles round the bath. 'I'll need my chisel and hammer. Well, don't just stand there,' he said, turning to glare at her standing shivering with bubbles bursting on her feet. 'I said get my chisel and hammer – I'll have to have the lot off!'

Silently she fetched the tools and went to get dressed. She touched the gilt handle of the wardrobe and the white door slid back to reveal her choice of garments in which to live out the day. There was the black cotton skirt sprigged with tiny flowers that she couldn't wear because she had worn it to a disastrous dinner at Julian's boss's when she had been secretly, she hoped, sick in the bathroom; there was the green dress in which she had failed her driving-test again; there was the yellow dress which she had mistakenly thought didn't need a petticoat and had been disabused of this notion by a group of Gas Board men digging in the town; the multi-coloured print that had looked so good in a neighbour's mail order catalogue and which Julian said made her look like a salad, in which she had inexplicably burst into tears at a Brownie coffee-morning, her poor red burst-tomato face working helplessly over a paper cup of coffee; the shimmering horror bought for the Rugby Club dance had died in the dustbin the next morning.

A round black, furry face looked round the bedroom door, green lamps dimmed for daylight stared at her, the mouth opened in a plaintive demand for breakfast. She picked up the cat and held him up next to her own face in the glass, observing bluish eyes in a pale face; black velvet, green glass, pink silk and deadly ivory. Loneliness dulls the eye, makes lank the hair. She turned heavily away from her reflection.

The sound of hammering and cracked ceramics falling into water came from the bathroom, then a strangled gurgle as Julian pulled out the plug. Then faintly over the spluttering of frying bacon came his voice from Bryony's bedroom.

'How many times have I told you to keep that animal off the bed?'

He came into the kitchen and scraped back a chair and sat down noisily, the tang of his aftershave mingling with the smell of coffee and bacon and an air-freshener which he had squirted in the bathroom and which was swirling in a cosmetic typhoon through the house.

'Why do we have a breakfast-room? he demanded.

'What do you mean?'

'I mean, why do we have breakfast in the kitchen? I mean a kitchen's for cooking in, a lounge is for lounging or relaxing in, a breakfast room is for breakfasting in. What's the point of my slaving my guts out in an attempt to create a standard of gracious living when you persist in behaving like a working-class slut? Where's Bryony?'

'I expect she's getting dressed.'

'You'd think she might make an effort to get down to breakfast on time. Sometimes I think she's deliberately avoiding me. Is this Flora margarine on the toast?'

'Yes.'

The silvery clang of the gate, Daisy had undercoated but not yet painted it, and a thump on the mat meant that the newspaper had arrived. Julian got up from the table to get it and returned, snapping it into his briefcase.

'I'm off. No toast for Bryony. If she can't be on time she gets no breakfast – starting from today. And don't waste it on the birds. Put it in the Rotocrop Accelerator. You can finish taking off those bathroom tiles and buy a large tub of Fix'n Grout. I'll choose the new tiles on Saturday.'

Daisy went to the window and waved a tea-towel at the departing car, more to check that he was safely off the premises than in a wifely farewell.

'Has he gone?' Bryony looked round the kitchen door.

'He's gone. Come and have your breakfast.'

When Julian came back unheard into the kitchen he couldn't believe his eyes and ears. Bryony appeared to be waving a piece of toast spread with jam and peanut butter to a pop song blaring from the radio and the cat was licking the sugary milk from a cereal bowl on the floor. Daisy turned from the sink, the song stilled on her lips and a smile falling from her face at his voice. He switched off the radio.

'I'm speechless,' he shouted. 'If I was to try to tell you what I feel at this betrayal of everything I've done for you it would take until the middle of next week. You seize every opportunity to undermine my authority. The grass needs cutting, that child's hair needs cutting, she looks like a tramp and if that pansy hairdresser you patronise charges you more than fifty pence to make hair look like a bird's nest it's daylight robbery. But that's beside the point – I came back to tell you that you'd better get a move on with those tiles because the Cluff-Trenches are coming to dinner next week. They'll expect a decent meal so you'd better buck up your culinary ideas. Sometimes I wonder what was the point of buying you that freezer. A chap at work has offered me a whole venison so I'll get him to bring it round. We can have some of it when the Cluff-Trenches come.'

'A whole venison?'

'Yes – a whole venison. You know what a venison is, don't you? One of those large animals with four legs and antlers,' he said with exaggerated patience.

'It wouldn't fit in?'

'What wouldn't fit in?'

'The venison wouldn't fit into the freezer. You'd have the antlers sticking out one end and the hind legs sticking out the other. Besides, they're deer.'

'Dear? Of course they're bloody dear! Do you think I can't afford the occasional venison on my salary? Besides he's letting me have it cheap. It was run over. As to its antlers you could cut them off and mount them on a plaque in the lounge.'

After he banged the front door for the second time that morning Julian looked up at his house for a moment. He was a junior partner in a firm of estate agents and it was his wish that at any given moment his property, as he called it even to himself, rather than house or even home, should merit the description 'Desirable residence in immaculate condition in sought-after area. Beautifully kept gardens'. Suppose he should be killed this morning and prospective buyers view his property before she had done the tiles or cut the grass? He almost turned back once more to tell her that there was a dandelion on the lawn and remind her to paint the gate but he had wasted enough time already.

'Remember this property's in my name,' he shouted as he got into the car. He wondered if he could have the words 'neglected by wife' added to the details. First some self-indulgent black person warbling on the radio and now some idle thrush making a noise in the lilac tree. He wound up the window and made the engine roar as he drove away.

The daffodils were gone, the cherry blossom gone, the lilacs crumbled in rusty cones, the irises withered to rags of crumpled silk and brown paper. The thrush which had offended Julian was still singing as Daisy walked part of the way to school with Bryony. They came to the stile where a friend awaited her. Daisy held her hand for a moment longer and kissed her. As the child ran ahead Daisy saw her again, still singing through her toast as Julian shouted at her in the kitchen, pyjama jacket unbuttoned, heartbeats pulsing, flickering faintly under the skin of her bare chest. She thought that a medal for gallantry should be pinned on that faded cotton pyjama jacket. Then came a vicious whisper above the bird's song and rustling buttercups. 'The murderess watches lovingly as her child walks to school.'

She turned and ran so that the noise of her feet and pounding heart would drown the voice.

'There is another mother who will never watch her children running through a summer field because of you.'

A heap of earth, a headstone bulked in her path. She tripped and grazed her knee and limped onto the little bridge and leaned on the rail, the river and the sunshine fusing in a silver curtain through unshed tears.

'Self-pity,' came the voice.

'If I don't feel sorry for myself – who will?' and that made the tears spill onto the wooden rail. A little flotilla of alder leaves and twigs was sailing down the brown water. An irridescent dragonfly bumped into her face. 'Get away, you great ugly helicopter,' she flapped at it, then watched it hover over a purple balsam and settle for a moment on a reed. Foolish to think she might have enjoyed the beauties of the day. The same black tentacles of the past that diminished and soured everything, that made her choose the least demanding, the most facile magazines, Bryony's comics, constant pop music on the radio, afternoon movies on television, lest anything make her think too much, had reached out and pulled her back.

Through the clear sky, slowly and inexorably a black cloud, on which sat the Cluff-Trenches eating a dead deer, pursued her. The little wood which had been bright and sunny with Bryony's chatter now seemed dark, full of sinister scrabblings and rustlings and unease.

She was not wrong in feeling uneasy in the wood, for a pair of eyes was watching through the slit in an old concrete pillbox left over from the war, half-buried in ivy and nettles.

As she chipped at the unrelenting tiles, realising that she would not dislodge half of them in a day, she composed an advertisement as if for insertion in the personal column of a newspaper: 'The ghost of Jennifer Greengrass. One who has wronged you, seeks to make amends.' Or: 'The late Jennifer Greengrass. One who wronged you seeks absolution. Please reply box no. –' How could you make amends to someone you had killed; had robbed of the chance to watch her children grow up? Guilt was like ground elder in the garden; you thought you had uprooted it and forgot about it for a while, then one day there it was, sprung up again, green and thriving, mocking all your efforts. Was she still as real to Jennifer Greengrass as Jennifer Greengrass was to her? Had she forgotten her or did she still hate her as much as when she had torn up Daisy's photograph and posted the pieces to her? Daphne had opened the envelope and the torn face fluttered like flakes of soot over their cold, disgraceful breakfast. If only. If only I hadn't.

Jennifer Greengrass was always at her side, casting her shadow over every pleasure, reminding her that she had no right to be happy. She had known her sentence the moment Julian's bristly mouth, for he was growing a moustache then, closed on hers like a harsh poisonous fruit. But it was what she deserved.

She could not, however, be accused of indulging in much happiness, except for an occasional unpreventable outbreak, like the sun suddenly piercing the cloud and illuminating the earth for a moment, inspired by her child. She was a dutiful if unenthusiastic housewife. Name-tapes, the whiteness of school socks and Julian's squash gear, correct dinner money, harvest festivals, school concerts and birthday parties were her preoccupations. When she and Julian and Bryony had first moved to Fairlawn, her kitchen calendar had been full of invitations to coffee-mornings and when she invited her hostesses back she would spend the day before in a fever of polishing and cutting fresh flowers and baking little delicacies to accompany the freshly-ground coffee. Word had got around that she was the daughter of Rex and Daphne Beaumont. Her new friends expected an introduction to 'La Vie Bohème' and invitations to literary parties at St Cloud where they could rub shoulders with the personalities from 'The Book Programme' and 'Call My Bluff'. When these were not forthcoming and they found that Daisy was as dull as themselves, they began to dislike her and call her 'stuck-up' and the invitations stopped.

The front-door chimes drilled through her, making her drop the chisel in the bath. Coloured bathroom suite, slightly damaged. She opened the door, still holding a piece of jagged tile. A woman in a headscarf stood on the step.

'Good morning, I wonder if you like many people are worried by the way things are going in the world today. Do you ever think about Eternity? May I ask if you've made Christ Jesus your personal saviour – oh no!'

'Not you!'

Esther Beaney, arch enemy, betrayer, blighter of her life turned *colporteuse*, stood on the step in a headscarf.

'Well, you seem to have fallen on your feet.'

Her small eyes glittered. Daisy noticed her hair under the scarf was still long, was tied back in a bit of chiffon. It was a rule of her sect that women should not cut their hair; her aunt had sported a long grey mare's tail to school functions. Esther had once told the girls that her uncle said a woman's crowning glory was her hair and Daisy had been stabbed with an inexplicable sadness, even as she pulled Esther's chair away and she sat down hard, bewildered, on the floor.

'Don't you know that's the most dangerous thing you can do?' cried Miss Windibank, pulling Esther from the floor, her dry neck flushing to the colour of her blouse. Now it seemed that she had willed the blouse to Esther or that Esther had found the religious outfitters where Miss Windibank bought her clothes.

'Aren't you going to ask me in?'

Daisy stepped back silently. Esther led the way. Daisy followed her like a zombie. Esther saw she had to take charge. 'Let's be cosy and sit in the kitchen. Now, where's the kettle? You don't mind Instant, do you?'

Daisy's mouth opened silently as Esther unhooked two mugs.

'Do sit down, you make the place untidy,' said Esther, clashing the spoon. A fine brown powder rose from the jar; Daisy felt she would choke; she sat down on a stool. The broken tile clattered to the floor. 'Black or white?'

'I prefer my coffee black, especially my own coffee in my own house!'

'So capitalism rears its ugly head. I thought you and Mr Greengrass were both communists, or was it Trotskyites? Has he seen the light too?'

'I've no idea what his politics are. I haven't seen or heard of him for years.'

'Of course, you don't keep in touch with the staff do you? Not that Mr Greengrass is on the staff any more, after your little escapade. I heard he had difficulty finding another job. Some of the girls were wondering if you'd turn up at Miss Darcy's Memorial Service, but you didn't, did you? Drink up – you look as if you'd seen a ghost. Sweetex? We gave her quite a good send-off. I rounded up a few of the old gang and suggested it would be a nice touch if we wore our ties as a token of respect, but unfortunately only Dopey Danvers and I had kept ours, and she turned up in the complete uniform and as she was pregnant the effect was disastrous, I mean – her tunic! Miss Windibank was furious and made her sit at the back. She really lowered the tone. You could hear her sobs right through the church. Miss Windibank had to leave her seat among the chief mourners and go to tell her to be quiet and in the end she gave her a hundred lines. Dopey said she wouldn't do them.'

'I bet she did though.'

Wasn't there some stuff you could get to paint over scratches in the bath? Daisy was wondering as she looked at Esther's hand. A gold ring indicated that someone had been foolish enough to join his life to hers and that she was Esther Beaney no more.

'I didn't know Miss Darcy was dead,' she said.

'There was a long obituary in the *Telegraph*.' Esther sounded huffy on their old headmistress's account.

'What carried her off in the end? Was it the halitosis or the dandruff or the hay-fever?'

'I shan't demean myself to answer those cheap cracks. No, Daisy, you remember it was her heart's desire to visit Oberammergau?'

'No.'

'Didn't you ever listen in Assembly? Well, anyway, she finally realised her dream and went to Oberammergau with Miss Windibank. No one will ever know what happened that day but Miss Windibank says that they were pulled apart by the crush of the crowd and the next time she saw Miss Darcy, she was astride a donkey, pursued by a group of Roman soldiers and then she was dragged from the dumb beast's back—'

'You don't mean she was cru . . .'

'Of course not! No, her poor old heart, her tired noble heart, simply gave up. They laid her lifeless on the stones. Miss Windibank strewed her with palms.'

'It's how she would have wanted to go,' murmured Daisy. '' 'The Donkey'' by Chesterton was always her favourite poem.'

'I'm glad you see it like that. She was due to retire. Her work here on earth was done and Our Lord called her to rest.'

'How is Our Lord these days? And Yahweh? Still keeping in touch, are you?'

Esther ignored this. 'We gave her a pretty good send-off. Miss Windibank did say she had hoped she might put in an appearance but she supposed even you wouldn't have the brass neck.'

'Brass neck?'

'She said she'd been doing a bit of detective work.'

Daisy saw two small white figures driven out of a green Eden by an angel with a fiery sword.

'Tracking down missing textbooks. She traced a copy of Maps of the Holy Land to you. You don't happen to have it handy do you?'

'No!'

'You've got a lovely home, Daisy, what does your hubby do?'

'Please go, Esther. Why have you come here like a bird of ill omen to haunt me with spectres of school? It's all so long ago and I don't care about any of it. "Take your beak from out my heart". As far as I'm concerned Miss Darcy and Miss Windibank and you are all ghosts.' And Jennifer Greengrass, she might have added.

Esther reassured herself with a finger that her nose was small and solid, as in days of yore.

'No need to get all aereated. I'll leave some literature with you and we can chat about it next time I call.'

She laid several smudgily duplicated leaflets on the table.

'Get out!'

'Right-o. I'll call back in a few days then. I could fit you in on Tuesday. No, I tell a lie – it might not be until Wednesday. Why are you crying? Is it something I said?'

'Just go.'

'Believe me, Daisy, I didn't come here to upset you. I thought it was just a routine call. I didn't even know you lived here. I've been away for several years on missionary work.'

She lunged forward and grasped Daisy's hand, squeezing the wedding ring painfully against her finger.

'There must be a purpose in our coming together. I have been sent to bring you to true repentance. Go on Daisy, have a good cry. Let the tears come – you'll feel better for it. I want you to know that I forgive you, and Jesus loves you.'

Daisy wrenched her hand away and threw her cold coffee full in Esther's face. Twelve years were washed away in an instant and the two girls glared at each other across a school dining-table, only this time it was custard that rolled down Esther's face.

Esther Beaney could draw a map of the Holy Land blindfold. She knew the difference between Jeroboam and Reheboam; her voice dropped a reverent semi-tone when she pronounced the name of Yahweh, which she did frequently. Rahab the harlot, Simon the tanner, Lydia a seller of purple slipped easily from her tongue; she licked her lips over the fates of Agag and Jezebel. The New Testament, however, was her forte; the classroom rang with her cries of 'Agape' and 'Eros' and 'the Seven Deacons'. 'Who the hell are the Seven Deacons?' muttered Daisy.

That she was on such intimate terms with 'Our Lord' was explained by the fact that she was a member of a sect, founded by her grandfather, which met on Lord's Day and several evenings a week in a green corrugated iron hut plastered with posters promising eternal damnation. The R.I. lesson was really a dialogue between Esther and Miss Windibank. The rest of the class got on with combing their hair, surreptitiously finishing homework, passing round the novels of Hank Janson, love-letters and photographs until Miss Windibank flew into one of her famous rages, and books and chalk flew about the room and her dry skin flamed to match her blouse.

Daisy, hitherto so quiet and biddable, began to achieve some notoriety. No one could think what had got into her. Her odd behaviour was noticed for the first time at a hockey match. The game was nineteen minutes into the second half; the red bands had the ball. Suddenly the centre-forward grabbed the referee's arm. 'Look!'

Way down the field, in the opposite goal mouth sat Daisy Beaumont, her padded legs stuck straight out in front of her, weeping hopelessly. 'The human condition' was all she would say when questioned. She was sent off.

Then, there was the English episode. 'One would have thought,' she half-heaved herself up in her desk, a languorous, insolent, sop to politeness, 'one should have thought that it might have been bad enough to be a housemaid, rising in the freezing dawn to clear out fires and black-lead grates and have red raw hands from primitive detergents through washing the plates of the over-fed privileged classes without people calling your soul damp.'

'That's quite enough, Daisy, sit down properly and take that ridiculous thing off your head. I will not have people coming to my classes improperly dressed.'

Daisy sank back and pushed the green eye-shade which, with a pair of steel armbands, she had worn since becoming the editrix of the school magazine, to the back of her head. A whisper went round the class that she had become a Communist.

'What's that? – I will not have my class disrupted! You . . . stand up and repeat what you have just whispered to your neighbour.' In a storm of giggles the girl managed to get out, 'I only said no wonder Daisy gets on so well with Mr Greengrass, seeing as they're both Communists,' before she was overcome and had to hide behind her *Modern Poetry for Schools*, from which a guffaw or two escaped. The mistress sighed and counted the minutes to the bell and the months until Daisy would leave school. Daisy fingered a packet of five Woodbines in her pocket and concentrated her attention on the sticky paper which had held a cream doughnut, which she had spread carefully on Esther's chair and which adhered pleasingly to her skirt.

At lunchtime in the canteen, with its primrose yellow melamine tables, Daisy felt disgust sweep over her in the babel of voices and scrape and clash of cutlery among her fellows, mouths opening on spoons, sucking in food like amoebas filling their vacuoles; a heap of tripe or wet wiping-up cloth lay at the side of the serving hatch. Daisy looked at Esther who sat opposite. Then she bent her head and sniffed appreciatively at her plate.

'I say, this custard smells good.'

The girls looked at her in disbelief.

'No really, go on, smell it!'

Esther duly bent forward and Daisy leaned over and pushed her face into the pudding. She sat up, spluttering indignantly with custard running down her face when Miss Windibank, attracted by the noise, materialised behind them.

'I was just smelling my custard . . .' Esther tried to explain.

'You were smelling your custard? What a disgracefully bad-mannered thing to do! Do you smell your custard at home? Go and apologise at once to the kitchen staff, then you can stand over there where everyone can see you!'

She stood, Esther Beaney, in her yellow shame.

Daisy cleared away the coffee cups and wiped spilt coffee from the floor. After school Bryony changed, which meant that she cast all her school clothes to the floor and swapped them for a pair of shorts and went out to play. As a little girl, Daisy's secret ambition had been to have a rose-wreathed cottage in the country, a tabby cat called Tibby, a budgie called Joey, a dog called Rover and ten children; the prototype for the girls having shiny yellow pigtails whose ribbons were never lost and neat white socks which stayed up without the aid of elastic bands biting the ankles or pins which scratched and pierced and made half-moons of blood soak into the turnovers. She had managed the cat who, however, was black and called Blacky; the budgie and dog had not been achieved. From the kitchen window she could see a pair of bare legs kicking in the tree. Her ideal children had been torn up like a row of paper dolls and replaced by one in a pair of cut-down jeans and nothing else, whose dark tangled mane hung loose over her brown back, who jumped over a fallen bicycle and ran off to play football, who raised tawny eyes to the window and smiled and waved a muddy hand, whose mother at this resisted an urge to seize the squirming body and smother it with kisses, and raised a hand in a sudsy salute and cried, 'Mind the road,' to the impoverished air.

'Mummy, there's a soldier in the wood and he's crying.'

A deserter. Wounded. On the run; armed.

'You children stay here; I'm going to investigate. You are not to follow me. Do you understand?'

She spoke so commandingly that Bryony and three small boys flattened themselves against the hedge. She snatched a plastic rifle from one of them.

She ran up the road, into the wood, and stopped at the head of the path. No one. Leaves and birdsong, the gurgling river. Then she pushed between two holly trees into the thicket and picked her way through brambles and nettles to the old pillbox that stood near the river bank. She stood in the dark doorway. A soldier was crouched in the corner, with his back to her.

'Turn around and put your hands up!' She prodded the rifle in his back. 'Walk!' He stumbled out.

In the sunlight she saw that he was not a soldier but a boy. His face tearstained. He took a step.

'Don't move! This is loaded.' She waved the black plastic rifle. A lolly stick fell from its muzzle.

'Oh well, it was loaded.' They both almost smiled.

'Why were you hiding there? Are you in trouble?'

He shook his head.

'Do you live round here? I think I've seen you before—'

'No.'

'Are you sure you're all right?'

She couldn't think what to say or do, but was reluctant to leave him.

'I was just going.'

'Where?'

'I don't know – anywhere.'

'You're on the run, aren't you?'

He nodded. 'I'm on the run. From the Army. In Ireland.'

'You're just a boy,' she said doubtfully.

'They're taking them younger these days.'

'I think you've run away from school. They have A.T.C.s in some schools, don't they?'

'O.T.C.' he said, then blushed as red as his hair as he realised his mistake.

'You'd better come home with me,' she said. 'I'll give you something to eat. I expect you're hungry.' She started to walk. As he followed she realised she had become responsible for him.

Bryony, Julian, the uncooked meal, the scratched bath awaited. She felt sick; the rifle was slippery in her hand. At every step she almost ran away. The day was still hot, thistle heads glittered and dazzled at the side of the flinty path. Having captured him, her mind searched wildly for ways to get rid of him. They reached the gate of Fairlawn in silence. She dared to look at the drive, dreading to see the car looming there, but the neat blue asphalt was bare and the open garage empty. The sound of the television came through a window. They crept into the kitchen. As she opened the fridge Daisy heard the car.

'My husband's home! You'll have to hide. Quick, go out the back door. There's a summer house in the garden. Hide there. I'll come out when I can. Go on – quick!' He was pushed back out of the door he had just come through; foodless.

Bryony's friends left as Julian came in; they seemed to melt away at his approach. Daisy heard Bryony's feet running to meet him in the hall, Julian's key, then his greeting, 'Mind your sticky fingers on my jacket.' Then a cry of anguish from the bathroom. The scratched bath.

The freezer came to the rescue. As the dinner thawed in the oven, Daisy watched in agony from the kitchen window as Julian pottered about in the garden, killing time by killing a few insects, dreading that at any minute he would turn towards the summer house. As he chewed his food a little muscle jumped at either side of his head. He looked tired and grey as he pushed away his plate. Daisy, thinking of the hungry boy outside, was unable to eat anything.

'Daddy, I'm in the 100 metres and the hurdles on Sports Day.'

'Make sure you win, then.'

'I was first in one of the practices in the hurdles, and second in the other and second in the 100 metres. Sally was first in the second

practice and Jane, no Wendy, was second and in the boys' hurdles
Richard—'

'I don't give a damn where Jane and Sally and Richard came! All
that matters is where you come on Sports Day, i.e. first. There's no
point in competing if you're not going to win. Remember that or
you'll never get anywhere in life.'

'Will you be able to come?'

Daisy couldn't tell which answer Bryony was hoping for.

'Of course I won't be able to come. I can't take time off to watch a
village school sports!'

Bryony smiled. 'Will you go in the Mums' race this year
Mummy?'

'Is there a Fathers' race?' demanded Julian at once.

Later from an upstairs window, Daisy saw him in the twilight
running round the lawn in his track suit, make an attempt to leap a
rosebed and fall in prickly defeat. There was no way that she could
carry sustenance to the summer house. After 'News at Ten' he
unplugged the television and switched out the light, which meant it
was time for bed. He heaved her over to his side of the bed but she
was on their honeymoon in Italy; kms and kms of oleanders on the
autostrada, speeding through endless tunnels to the campsite; those
three dead dogs, huge, raw, hit by car after car, which must have
been thrown there; in a field beside a country road a cow rolling on
its side with a soft bundle of hooves sticking out of it. She had
begged Julian to stop but he neither heard nor saw. She had
imagined in an instant running to the farmhouse, while Julian
revved the car impatiently, trying frantically to explain to the farmer
in English that one of his cows was in labour, in distress, but instead
she sank back in her seat in weakness, in defeat. Now, years later as
she lay at the edge of sleep a picture of a very small soldier, with a
chafed neck, swam into her mind.

She woke an hour later to the immediate awareness that it was
raining. Julian's snores cut through the darkness like a mower on a
black lawn. She lay for a few moments, then eased down the bed,
inch by inch until her feet touched the floor. She stood for a few
minutes, waiting for a break in Julian's breathing. He slept on. It
took her some time to open the door and close it behind her. Once
outside it, she felt her way on tip-toe along the wall and crept like a
thief to a cupboard where she dragged out a slithery sleeping bag. It
gasped and floundered in her arms like a great fish as she carried it

downstairs and tried to trip her up. She would not have been surprised if it had opened its zip and cried, as in a fairy tale, 'Master, Master, someone is stealing me!'

She had to switch on the kitchen light and laid the sleeping-bag on the floor while she grabbed some bread and cheese and a bottle of milk, then she unlocked the back door, put off the light and went out into the night with her spoils. Her feet were numb in the wet grass before she reached the summer house, rain hammering on her thin nightdress. Black roses reached out to claw her as she knocked with her elbow, her hands being full, on the wooden door.

'Open the door. It's me,' she hissed.

Silence and darkness within beat on the wooden walls; outside, swishing and dripping rain.

'Oh, hurry up,' she moaned. 'Open the door!' She kicked at it again and again. At last it opened and she thrust the wet bundle at the dark figure standing there and turned and ran, expecting at any moment to see the house flooded with light and Julian silhouetted in the doorway. She got in safely, however, and rubbed her hair a little with the bathroom towel before crawling back into bed. Julian sat up suddenly, still asleep, drew back a somnolent fist and punched at her, then turned over and resumed snoring.

When she woke he was already up. It was not until she pulled back the covers and saw her feet black with dried mud and a little slug nestling under her ankle that she remembered her night adventure. She closed her eyes again but the boy soldier, Esther Beaney, Jennifer Greengrass, her lonely, unwritten-to mother-in-law all stood at the bedhead welcoming her to another day. She rose and placed the slug temporarily in the leaves of a spider plant and stuffed the muddy sheet in the linen basket.

At nine-fifteen she went down to the summer house. He was sitting up with the sleeping bag round his shoulders. The milk bottle was empty.

'Thank you for the food,' he said. 'And the sleeping bag. I was freezing.'

'I'm sorry I couldn't come earlier.'

'That's all right. You saved my life.'

'Good.' She glanced round; some plants in pots on the shelves, empty flower pots, a rake, a pair of gardening gloves, a crumpled bread wrapper.

'I feel rather like Googie Withers in "It Always Rains on Sundays".'

'And I feel like Tommy Swan in the air raid shelter.'

'I didn't think you'd know what I was talking about.'

'I've seen more old movies that you've had hot dinners,' he boasted, then looked abashed.

'Anyway, the coast's clear,' said Daisy, dismissing a shared taste for, or escape, into afternoon movies on television.

They picked their way through the wet grass to the house. There was a slight scuffle at the back door as he stepped back to let Daisy go in first and to remove his boots.

'Your feet!' cried Daisy.

He looked down at them, red and blistered on the shiny tiles. He heard her running upstairs; then she came back with a pair of slippers. He put them on; they were gentle and warm, caressing his feet.

'I've never worn slippers before. They're quite nice, aren't they?'

'Do sit down.'

He sat on a stool, while she made coffee and toast, and looked nervously at the glittering steel and formica. He had never been in a kitchen like this. There was a fridge and a washing machine and a blender; all the cups hung neatly on hooks; a shelf of cookery books, a spice rack, a glass dish of green peppers and aubergines and a purple cabbage; but where was the sludge behind the taps, the cruddy milk, the pile of clothes for the launderette, the ashtray? Daisy took eggs from a shallow yellow earthenware dish and fried them in a green pan. The smell of toast and coffee brought tears to his eyes. Daisy decided to let him eat before questioning him, then had a sudden thought. 'Shall I show you the bathroom before you eat?'

When he returned the food was on the table, eggs and coffee, followed by a small hill of toast, silvery with butter, to be spread with home-made marmalade. She sat, drinking coffee from a flowery mug, watching him eat.

'That was great. Thank you very much.'

Daisy sat down on the beechwood stool and looked at him, his khaki trousers which bagged rather poignantly at the seat.

'Well, what am I to do with you? If you were David Copperfield and I was Betsy Trotwood I'd give you one of my old dresses to wear, wouldn't I?'

'Miaow,' said Blacky in the doorway.

'Mr Dick sets us all right,' said Daisy. 'I'll get you some of Julian's things while I wash yours.'

45

'Don't bother, these are O.K.'

'It's no bother.'

He tried to postpone the inquisition he knew was coming. He patted his pockets.

'You haven't got a cigarette, have you?'

'No. Well, that is, my husband's got some he keeps for guests.' She went out again and came back with a packet and a Wedgwood table lighter. She offered him one. He took the pack from her and offered it to her. Touched by this courtesy she took a cigarette. He lit it and then his own. She wondered who had taught him to do that. A fly alighted on the lip of the milk jug; she waved it away and it buzzed off to join three others circling round the light.

'I'm sorry about the flies. I don't like to kill them, although I suppose one should. My husband . . .'

'My Mum,' he began, then blushed and stopped.

'Yes, your Mum. What about your Mum? Won't she be worried sick?'

'She won't know. She's in Ireland.'

'Like you were in Ireland?'

'No. She really is in Ireland. She's gone to Dublin with her boyfriend.'

'Oh!'

'Anyway she knows I can take care of myself.'

'Your father, then?'

'I haven't got a father. At least, I have, – but I never see him. He's married.'

'Oh!' said Daisy again, then, 'Are you sure your mother's in Dublin?'

He pulled some pieces of a postcard from his pocket and handed them to her. She put them together on the table and saw a Dublin postmark and read: 'We are afloat on seas of whisky but keeping our heads above the surface. Love Ma.'

Unable to think of anything to say she turned the bits over and discovered the mummified body of a nun.

'Why is it torn up?'

'A boy at school did it, so I hit him, only he was supposed to be an officer so I left. I never wanted to go there anyway.'

'Was he badly hurt, this boy? You didn't injure him, did you?'

'No, he was all right; just a bit concussed I suppose. I just couldn't stick it any more.'

'Have you any brothers and sisters, then?'

'I've got a sister somewhere, only I've never met her. A half-sister but she doesn't want to know me.'

'Oh dear' said Daisy, 'I don't know what to do. I don't suppose you'd consider going back to school?'

She fiddled with the bits of torn card, as if by putting it together, like a jigsaw, she would solve the problem. She couldn't imagine herself sending such a postcard to Bryony. She felt angry with his feckless mother. Fancy sending such a card to school, to be sneered at by the other boys. And his uncaring father and sister. She recalled fleetingly her own inauspicious exit from school. Then she realised he was trying to force a muddy boot onto his foot.

'Don't do that. I'll think of something.'

He stopped at once. What would she think of? There were dishes to be done, washing, shopping, tiles to be removed. Perhaps his story was a tissue of lies, but she didn't think it was. Anyway she had no alternative but to believe it.

'What's your name?'

'Seamus.'

That at least rang true – the red hair, the references to Ireland.

'Seamus what?'

'Kavanagh. Or Beaumont. My mother's name is Kavanagh but she changed it to Mandrake. She's a poet.'

'Beaumont? That's funny. My name used to be Beaumont.'

'Did it? I usually use the name Kavanagh because my father doesn't like me to use his name. He's a writer. You might know him, he lives round here. Only I'm not supposed to tell people he's my father. What's up?'

She was sitting staring in front of her, her face had gone all white. 'Shut up a minute! Sorry. I think we may be, I know this sounds mad, but I think we might be cousins. No, it's impossible, he's not married. You don't mean Stanley Beaumont's your father, do you?'

'Rex Beaumont.'

■ CHAPTER FIVE ■

'I forgot to tell you,' said Daphne, 'I saw Stanley the other day in Sainsbury's. He looked awful.'

'Always does,' said Rex.

'His basket was pathetic – a tin of beans, one orange and a shaving stick, a shabby little bachelor basket. The strange thing was, he had a child with him. A rather beautiful little boy, but very dirty. You don't suppose he's taken up with some woman, do you? It couldn't be his, I suppose?'

'It's his landlady's child; he takes it about with him sometimes. Savage little brute, name of Jason I believe. It bit me once outside the library.'

'Poor Stanley. I must ask him to supper soon. I'll ask Daisy too. We'll have a real family get-together. I suppose Julian will have to come. He gets more and more unpleasant. Really I can scarcely bear to breathe the same air as him. Thank goodness Daisy still adores him though. I'll ring her now. Finchy can drop a note into Stanley when she's in town. Why do you sigh? Don't you want to see your family? You're a most unnatural man. Really, if it wasn't for me I doubt if you'd ever see them at all. Do you think that if I'd married Stanley you'd have become him and he'd have become you, if you see what I mean? I wonder if you draw your strength from me, like mistletoe growing on an apple tree?'

'If you are planning, as I saw at once that you are from the way your eyes lit up when you said that, to write a story about us entitled "The Mistletoe on the Apple Tree", you can forget it!'

As Daphne left the room he heard her murmur, 'The Mistletoe on the Apple Tree, Mistletoe and Apple Bough'. Her head popped back round the door.

'The Ivy and the Oak!'

How on earth could she think that Daisy adored Julian? Self-delusion. Self-delusion. He turned on the radio and strode about the room, picked up and gazed into a paperweight, a pansy

48

embalmed in glass. Shame was setting up the projector and selecting a cine film. Rex headed the disgraceful procession along the rusted railway track, taken over by sorrel and ragwort; white fluff from ripening willowherb floated on the hot air and clung to their clothes; Rex, Daphne, Mrs Finch, Miss Darcy in silent single file swishing through the weeds, an incongrous avenging train pulling into the axed station, mounting the deserted platform and crashing into the old station master's house where Daisy and Tom Greengrass, her erstwhile art master, sat at a table. Beans fell from their forks. Behind the hills tinted red and purple with ripening dogwood and wayfaring trees visible through the open window, Jennifer Greengrass lay in a hospital bed facing their reverse slopes blindly through an overdose. There was a drawing of Daisy, propped against a milk bottle holding a spray of rowan berries. Daphne snatched it and tore it into pieces that drifted onto the dusty floor, were tossed into a little white snowstorm by one of Miss Darcy's sneezes; with swollen and streaming eyes she had braved the battalions of pollen and grass seed that attacked her sensitive nasal membranes, a martyr in the cause of righteousness. It was Mrs Finch, acting on information from one Esther Beaney, who had somehow sniffed out the hideaway of the guilty pair and telephoned the school. Rex wished now that he had the drawing, those tender pencil-strokes; it was the only picture he had seen in which his daughter looked happy. Daphne had hurled, too, in shameful confetti, a torn-up photograph at the illicit bride. And now he supposed he had sold Seamus down the river too. Shame the projectionist selected another slide; Rex, tiny pink bubbles still fizzing his brain, had paused, one autumn night after a party, outside an amusement arcade in the Tottenham Court Road and a boy, attracted by the velvet lapels of his coat and expensive scent, had invited him for a cup of coffee. Rex hailed a taxi, closing the windows against the alluring night and the moon old and wicked in the purple sky above the glittering Post Office Tower, and fled to the safety of Surrey. The boy was about Seamus's age.

He looked down at his hand and opened his fist to see that he was clenching the paperweight and that it had printed a deep hexagon on his palm. News of a traffic accident came from the radio; a coach carrying holiday-makers had crashed over a cliff. If Julian and Mrs Finch and Maud could be prevailed upon to take a trip together in a coach steered by a drunken driver . . . He could bring Daisy and

Bryony and Seamus to St Cloud where they could live happily ever after. Except of course, for Stanley. He booked a ticket for Stanley on the doomed coach and made a tentative reservation for Daphne in the adjoining seat.

He would turn a blind eye to the cans of coke jostling their garish shoulders between the Meissen and jade on the marble mantlepiece, the motorbikes churning up the gravel. He might hire a girl from the village to help with the heavy work, a simple, accommodating maiden whom nature had deprived of speech but compensated with other gifts.

The music buzzing softly on the radio was drowned by another poignant little tune. Daisy at the piano, mirrored in glowing rosewood, the black notes clotted on the creamy paper of her book, her hair falling in a molten stream down her straight slender back as she struck the plangent notes of Czerny's "Sunday morning".

Daphne re-entered. 'I've mislaid my emerald ring.'

'Well, you said you wanted to lose a stone, though why I don't know – you're as skinny as a rake. I mean, you're perfect as you are.'

'Here it is! On the table – look.'

The stone swam in a tear, blurred green and gold rays. Rex wiped his eye.

'What was that tune you were singing as I came in?'

'Was I? I don't know!'

'Wasn't it something Daisy used to play?'

'It was nothing. A ghostly hand just brushed the rusty strings of my heart and they emitted a harsh jangling sound.'

'You never could sing in tune. What was it though, Rex?'

'I haven't the faintest idea.' He turned away to open the piano, which bared its yellow neglected teeth reproachfully, and dropped the lid. Daphne winced as though he had dropped it on her fingers. She went in search of Mrs Finch who was disembowelling a fowl, but turned back.

'Have you heard again from Maud?'

'No.'

'I expect he's turned up then.'

No banns had been called for Daisy's wedding, so Rex had not been able, as he had often fantasised since the misalliance, to stand up in chuch and declare:

'I forbid the banns!'

The noose had been tied in the Register Office one May morning when cowparsley and hawthorn blossom frothed like champagne in the hedges, a perfect day for a wedding, and there was no just cause or impediment why those two people should not be joined together in holy matrimony, except that Julian was a nasty little twerp and Daisy was probably marrying him to spite her father, who wept throughout the ceremony, flanked by Daphne who was looking on the bright side through a rose-coloured veil and Stanley who had opted to wear plimsolls for the occasion. Julian's mother, whom Rex had not seen since, had travelled up by train from Eastbourne that morning and taken advantage of the ladies' room at the station to soak herself in the scent of ersatz violets; she stood on Stanley's right, a carnation in silver paper pierced by the pin of the glass brooch, on her lapel, in the shape of a ruby-bodied spider. Julian had scorned the offices of the church, being unable, Rex supposed, to imagine the existence of a Being who was not listed in any of the Readers Digest Handbooks which formed his library.

Yet again the blame could be laid at Rex's door. If he had not, on a whim, between books, decided to have St Cloud valued to assess its market price, although he would sooner have had his golden hairs plucked out one by one than sell a brick or blade of grass of it, that hateful little M.G. would have never scrunched up the drive and sounded a rude blast on its horn as its owner vaulted over the side to get his foot in the door of St Cloud and suggest a programme of modernisation which involved, among other improvements, knocking down walls to give a through-lounge and replacing the windows, each of which made a dozen pretty frames for garden, birds and sky, with vast blank aluminium-edged so-called picture windows and sliding doors which would give onto a patio paved with slabs coloured pink and green and yellow like giant dog biscuits; and eventually carry off pale, submissive Daisy, too bored and guilty to refuse any longer his importunings, to the lights of Dorking glittering in the valley below.

■ CHAPTER SIX ■

Julian was having a rotten day; he had woken with a headache from a dream and lay beside the sleeping Daisy trying to piece it together. It was the school Sports Day. He had won the Fathers' race but when he went up to get his prize no one applauded. He was praying for someone to clap, sweating, looking round the crowd, almost begging for a friendly face. As he walked up to the table he thought that he would make a dazzling speech and win them over, then someone started a slow handclap.

'In view of your apparent unpopularity we have decided to ask your wife to accept the award on your behalf and I must ask you to submit to a saliva test.'

He wondered if his shouts had woken him; they had not apparently woken Daisy, he thought bitterly. He could scream all night and she would not hear him. Naturally she had not come to his rescue. One thing was certain; he would not be going to any school Sports Day.

Still heavy with bad dreams, he pulled into the cobbled courtyard behind Cluff-Trench and Spink, Estate Agents, to which he had been transferred some years ago from the Eastbourne branch, and his head began to throb when he learned that two junior members of the staff were malingering and that he would have to show a prospective buyer round two properties. A pretty girl, new to the office, in her first job, was hovering with his coffee. He stared at her checked dress and boots.

'That outfit is more appropriate to a wild west saloon than a business establishment. Try to wear something more suitable tomorrow. Oh! for God's sake, don't cry into my coffee. And get me some aspirin.' She rushed out. He thought he caught Mrs Jobson, Mr Cluff-Trench's P.A., mouthing 'pompous twit' through her red lipstick. He had to keep in with Mrs Jobson, for she had Mr Cluff-Trench's ear.

'These young girls!' he sighed humorously. 'Perhaps you could give her some tips on suitable office wear, Mrs Jobson?'

Too late he remembered that Mrs Jobson had worn an almost identical outfit yesterday.

'I couldn't find any aspirin, Mr Almond. Will paracetamol do?'

'That's fine, er, dear – thank you.'

He swallowed two white tablets with his coffee. He remembered a joke Bryony had once told him.

'I say, er Jane, do you know why you can't get aspirin in the jungle?'

'I don't know, Mr Almond.'

'Because the paracetamol! Ha-ha! Get it?'

'I take it it's a play on words, Mr Almond. Parrots eat'em all. Paronomasia.'

'Yes, well, thank you, Jane. Get me the details of the Henderson property.'

Silly little cow, flaunting her 'O' level English. Anyway what had persecution mania got to do with his joke? Or was it a disease you got from parrots? Then, like the sun bursting through a cloud, came Mrs Jobson's laugh, warm and beatific.

'I thought that was rather good, Mr Almond. The old jokes are the best jokes, eh?'

Jane placed the file on his desk and hovered again.

'Mr Almond?'

'What is it, Jane?'

'My name's not Jane, Mr Almond. It's Jenni. With an "i".'

'Of course.'

How he disliked those ruched ankle boots. A shapely calf, a neatly-shod foot, a trim ankle. These were phrases that gave him a faint frisson. He shrugged over his coffee, trying to shift the dull permanent ache of loneliness that had settled years ago between his shoulder blades.

Julian arrived early at the Henderson property and his ill-humour was not enhanced by its mean terraced aspect. He couldn't understand how it had got onto their books. It had belonged to an old lady, who had died and it was being sold by her nephew. He stood on the pavement fingering its key in his pocket, staring at the rotten window frames. A tiny boy on a yellow bicycle fitted with stabilisers trundled towards him.

'My brother's got the measles,' he said.

'Good,' said Julian.

The boy turned his vehicle round and pedalled furiously for home, ringing his bell wildly in alarm and disbelief.

Julian was turning the key in the lock of the empty house when he heard the gate click behind him.

'I hope you haven't been waiting long,' came from one half of what could only be described as a young couple, evidently soon to become a young trio.

'The bus was late,' explained the female section breathlessly.

'Not to worry, Madam.'

The headache was beating like a muffled drum over his eye. Passage through the little rooms was made difficult by the fact that the young couple held hands, tightly. All three banged heads once when Julian drew their attention to a power point in the kitchen. The husband had obviously read a manual on house purchase. He started to show off with talk of damp-courses and air-bricks and ring mains.

'Of course,' Julian turned to tell them on the narrow staircase, 'this property has been rather neglected owing to the previous owner's age and ill-health, hence the reasonable price, but it has enormous potential. Sound as a bell, these old properties – they don't build them like this any more.'

They stood in the front bedroom, inhaling a sharp odour of cats. A wardrobe stood on the bare boards against the dark flowered wallpaper which was browned with age. They all stared at it. Julian managed to push up the stiff window, which obviously hadn't been opened for years.

'Marvellous view of the North Downs!' he said.

They followed him obediently to the window.

'Marvellous view,' said the husband.

'Marvellous,' echoed the wife, but turned at once to the wardrobe.

'Let's have a look at the other bedroom,' suggested Julian hastily, starting to lead them through. 'You mustn't judge it as it is – you must imagine it nicely decorated, with a nice washable Vymura wallpaper for instance and a nice modern bedroom suite, padded headboard and matching units.' For the first time, the girl detached her hand from her husband's and ran to the wardrobe and pulled open the door. A heap of silk dresses like dead old ladies slithered to the floor. She burst into tears.

'I'm sorry,' she sobbed, searching her sleeve for a tissue. 'It was seeing her clothes like that. It just upset me.' The husband put his arm round her.

'It's because she's expecting,' he explained. 'It makes her a bit morbid.'

'I get a bit morbid,' she agreed. 'I know I do, but I can't help it. It's because I'm expecting. It was seeing her clothes, like – I don't like to think about things like d-d-d—.' The rest of her words were lost in the tissue.

The husband pulled a large snowy handkerchief from his oily jeans and dabbed at her eyes. 'Come on, gel, big blow.'

She obeyed him. Julian averted his eyes to the North Downs.

'I think we'd best be going,' the husband said. 'Sorry, mate. Thanks for your trouble.'

'Don't decide too hastily,' said Julian. 'Think it over for a day or two, but don't leave it too long or you might lose it. The vendor's anxious to make a quick sale. It's the perfect house for a first-time buyer and when you increase your family,' he bared his teeth in a respectful smile at the front of her dress, 'you can either extend, there should be no problem with planning permission, or sell at a profit and move on to something a little more up-market. Personally I think this room could be ideal for a baby, with a nice nursery wallpaper and—'

'My baby's not going in that room where – she . . . she . . .'

'Ta-ta, mate. Thanks.'

They clattered down the uncarpeted stairs. Julian, left alone in the room where the old lady had died, scooped up the dresses, heavy and slippery in his arms. A brown moth fluttered out and fell to the floor. He bundled them into the wardrobe and kicked the door shut. It swung slowly open and a black sleeve slid out. He turned and ran downstairs and locked the front door behind him. He stood in the dank little garden, taking deep breaths, staring into a clump of persicaria blooming over the drain. He did not know its name or that it was one of the many species of flora and fauna and birds that happened to be at the crucifixion, hence the dark spots on its leaves, only that its flowers, like pink silk french knots, reminded him of another dismal terraced house in Eastbourne that he preferred to forget.

As he drove away he reassured himself with the image of Fairlawn in its green sward. Fairlawn was fair enough for the present, but he wanted St Cloud.

He overtook the young couple and stopped and wound down the window. 'What about the other property you wanted to view?'

'Some other time, mate.'

As amber showed, Julian shot forward. He always liked to be first away at the lights, and had to slam on the brake. An old fool had decided to chance her luck; Mrs Finch, crammed into one of his mother-in-law's cast-off dresses. Julian sounded his horn loudly, making passers-by turn to look at her scuttling to the opposite pavement. It was on the night of Bryony's birth that Mrs Finch had destroyed his happiness. The proud father and grandparents and Mrs Finch, who was almost part of the family, were wetting the baby's head in the drawing-room of St Cloud whose stained glass window had absorbed the night sky which dyed its pale panes inky-blue and green. Rex poured the champagne.

'Thank you, Father,' said Julian, taking his glass and calling someone that name for the first time in his life. He smiled round their little circle, at Rex, Daphne, at old Finchy who was saying that she hoped she wouldn't get squiffy.

'Well, it's not every day we become grandparents,' Daphne encouraged her.

'Cheers then. Long life and happiness to all.'

Mrs Finch raised the glass tulip to her lips, sneezed and added, 'Well, we never thought we'd be standing here drinking champers the night young Daisy run off with that art teacher, did we?'

The champagne turned to acid in Julian's glass, and corroded everything. He never called Rex 'Father' again.

Now he decided to have a quick one, before going back to the office. He leaned across the bar which smelled of disinfectant and wet ashtrays and said to the barmaid, 'I'd like to pass a law making it compulsory for people to maintain their property up to standard. Trained inspectors to check the pointing and flashing and grouting and the timbers for dry rot, wet rot, damp etc., and if the owner was convicted of not redecorating thoroughly, interior and exterior, every five years, he would be subject to a heavy fine. For a first offence. Thereafter he would be put up against a wall and shot. People like that make me physically sick!'

'Oh, I do agree!' concurred the barmaid heartily. She couldn't know that it was Rex's head he saw blasted open with a volley of bullets.

'To me, flaking paintwork on a window-frame looks as bad as chipped nail varnish on a woman's hand,' added Julian. She hid her hands under the counter.

'Why has she moved away?' thought Julian. 'Why do I feel so bloody miserable all the time? The more I get, the more it feels like nothing.' He thought of his parents-in-law writing their silly books while that beautiful house fell into rack and ruin. It would need thousands spent on it by the time he got it. If he got it. They didn't even bother to pretend to like him now; he wondered if they ever had. They were probably just grateful to get Daisy off their hands. He could sometimes feel almost sorry for her. They were the most self-centred people he had ever met, with their clever remarks and jokes he didn't understand, and the way their eyes slid off you. And they were too tall.

And yet he had been happy at first. He had thought he had found a family; rich, handsome, sophisticated; cut glass, silver and candlelight. Then there was Fairlawn, which Rex had helped him to buy, Daisy, and the baby. He had mistaken Daisy's despair for modesty. He had thought of her as a cool white flower, more a lily, who might bruise at his touch. 'Lilies that fester,' he said as he finished his drink.

▪ CHAPTER SEVEN ▪

Mrs Finch didn't see why she should be expected to act as messenger boy for Lady Muck, in addition to all her other duties. She had no time for Stanley. Of course, he couldn't be telephoned like any normal person; oh no, she had to go traipsing round Dorking after doing the shopping, to stick notes through his door, missing the third part of 'Crown Court' most probably. It was funny how they deliberately seemed to make her miss the verdict every week. The number of times she had seen parts one and two and then just as somebody was about to be sentenced one of them would ring that blessed bell as if on purpose. In addition too, this dress was really badly cut. No wonder Lady Muck had palmed it off on her. She was perspiring like a pig. She tried to remember if Baconbonce had perspired much but it was too long ago. Mrs Finch did not single Daphne out for special disapprobation; in fact she was fonder of her and Rex than of anyone. People, trees, clouds, flowers, animals, stars, seas, dreams, ambitions, love all came under her scorn. She just thought the universe a very silly scheme and would tell its creator so to his face. For she believed in speaking her mind, although in the event she would probably express her disapproval within a series of withering sniffs like those she was uttering now as she approached Hope Villa. Two friends, elderly ladies in trousers, grey speckled socks and hiking boots, approached her and asked the best way to Box Hill.

'I wouldn't know,' said Mrs Finch, staring resolutely at its wooded slope. They crunched timidly away.

She had to pick her way past a series of expensive toys rusting on the broken path. Some people had more money than sense. The sound of a television came through the front room window. Mrs Finch pressed the bell. There was no reply. She rang again. Then she saw that the door was slightly open and gave it a little kick. It swung back and she could hear clearly the beginning of 'Crown Court'.

'Ooh – ooh,' she called. 'Anybody home?'

No one but the television. She looked round furtively and pushed open the front-room door. A huge television stood in the corner, and opposite it, on the vinyl sofa, lay a little boy, fast asleep, clutching a dirty piece of blanket. Mrs Finch tiptoed over to the set, adjusted the colour, and settled herself in a chair with her feet on a pouffe. She nodded in agreement with the prosecuting counsel. At this point Jason stirred and, sensing something amiss, sat up. 'I want my Nan!' he wailed.

'Shut up!' said Mrs Finch. 'You're asking for a smack.'

He subsided, whimpering. As she turned back to the screen a glitter of bottles caught her eye. She poured herself a strong one and settled back.

'Well, she got what she deserved!' remarked Mrs Finch with satisfaction after the verdict as she rose reluctantly to go. She was half-way down the path before she remembered the point of her journey and had to turn back to thrust Daphne's note through the letter box but could not, of course, see a little hand pick it up, examine it, and stuff it disdainfully into a plastic pillar box. Everything looked slightly odd, as if someone had turned the colour up too high. She had swallowed her gin too quickly. She found herself thinking about the old days, as she did rarely now, when her husband had fallen under a tractor and she had moved into St Cloud. Her gratitude had soon evaporated. Obviously it suited them better to have a permanent baby-sitter and they had only done it for their own advantage. A hiccup sounded loudly in the empty street. She looked round to see who had done it. Stanley lay on his bed listening to his thudding heart. A bag of books spilled out beside him. He was obviously losing his mind. The madness which lay in wait for him had sprung out. He had started to hallucinate. He had been on his way out when he thought he had seen old Finchy sprawled in a chair with her feet on a pouffe and a glass of gin in her hand, watching 'Crown Court'. If this was insanity, how dull! Must he now expect her to pop up at bus-stops, behind shop-counters, at the library, in the bathroom? Electrocuted by this last thought, he sprang off the bed and stood trembling. Jason stood in the doorway trailing his blanket.

'You, too!' gasped Stanley. 'What have I done? Why are you haunting me? Why are you staring at me? I know it's not really you. The real Jason has gone out. You're just a phantom conjured up by my sick brain.'

The phantom stood and stared.

'Go away. Begone!' cried Stanley, rushing at it, waving his arms.

The apparition let out a very earthly wail.

Stanley, laughing with relief, seized it and lifting it up, covered its surprised head with kisses.

'What do you think you're doing? Put him down at once!'

Mrs Herring, rubescent, swelling with outrage and salacious thoughts, pulled Jason roughly from Stanley's arms.

'Get downstairs, Jason!'

'I don't know what you were up to, and I don't want to know but I'm warning you, if I ever see you lay a finger on my grandson again, it's a police matter.'

'I thought you had taken Jason out,' was all Stanley could say.

'I was going to, only he was asleep. I was only gone five minutes,' she lied. 'Good thing I was, from the look of things when I came in. While the cat's away!'

'Oh God,' said Stanley, sitting down heavily on the bed.

He spent twenty minutes convincing her that he had no designs on Jason. He restrained himself with difficulty from adding that Jason was a repulsive little nuisance, who was ruining what was left of his life. She left at last, professing herself satisfied, perhaps weighing Stanley's usefulness as a babysitter and childminder against his suspected unnatural tendencies.

'He's like the grandson I'll never have,' said Stanley and, seeing himself acquitted, asked if she needed anything from the shops, as he was just going out.

'You can get me a nice piece of liver and take Jason if you like.'

Stanley was suitably grateful. They set off together. They stopped to buy Jason an ice cream. He spent an inordinately long time studying the pictures on the side of the fridge. Stanley studied the prices. 'The mini-milk looks rather good,' he suggested.

'Too little,' said Jason.

'What about an Orange Fizz?'

'I want a Cornetto.'

'But they're thirty-five pence.'

'You said I could choose.'

'Within limits – that's seven shillings in old money.'

'I want a Cornetto.' Jason started to stamp.

'He knows his own mind,' chuckled the woman behind the counter. Stanley sighed and paid up.

'Just one Cornetto, give it to me,' the woman trilled to the tune of 'Oh Sole Mio' as in the television advertisement, as she handed Jason his prize.

'Terrible, isn't it,' she commiserated as she took the money, ensuring Stanley a nicotine-free evening. 'I remember when we used to get an ice cream and a bag of sweets and still get change from a half-penny, don't you?'

'No,' said Stanley.

They paused for a moment outside a little junk shop. Among the unwanted objects jumbled in the window stood a lustre jug covered with a circlet of cream lace edged with green beads. It struck a chord in Stanley's memory. His grandmother had had just such a lace cover to keep the flies off the milk. If she had judged Stanley the poor creature his parents thought him, she gave no sign. It seemed that she alone saw no difference between Stanley and Rex, the little golden-headed King on mummy's knee. Jason fished in his back pocket and brought out a packet of sweet cigarettes. The green beads wobbled.

'Why are you cryin'?'

Stanley looked down at the candy fag sticking out of his chocolate-smeared rosy mouth.

'Because you've got cigarettes and I haven't.'

As Jason squatted in the sawdust in the butcher's, he suddenly looked up from the castle he was building and remarked.

'It's your own fault.'

'What's my own fault?'

'Well, you should of buyed some cigarettes for yourself so it's your own fault.'

'Yes,' said Stanley, receiving a limp parcel. 'Of course it's my fault. Everything that has gone wrong from the dawn of time is my fault.'

He barged blindly into half a cow.

'Sorry,' he said. 'My fault.'

Mrs Finch materialised again in the library – at least her voice came clearly through the book-lined ether:

'That *Crime and Punishment* book you gave me last time wasn't much cop. Very long-winded; have you got anything in the True Confessions series?'

'We've got *Confessions of an Opium Eater*.'

'I'll give it a try.'

When Stanley dared peek through the shelf there was no one there.

■ CHAPTER EIGHT ■

'I never knew I was an uncle,' said Seamus. 'It seems funny, being an uncle for years and not knowing it.'

Daisy sat dumb with guilt opposite the red-haired brother she hadn't known about.

'I must've been six when she was born. I wonder what I was doing then? I must've been in Ireland. I used to live there for a bit with my grandparents.'

'Were you happy?' asked Daisy.

'Yes, I liked it better than London but I was only young then.'

'Do you still see your grandparents? Go back for holidays?'

'No. They're both dead.'

'Oh dear!'

The green idylls she hoped for dissolved.

'Are you a writer?'

'No, I'm just a – no. Would you like some more coffee?'

'Yes, please.'

Daisy felt she should say something nice about his mother's work, although what she had read of it seemed self-indulgent nonsense. She planned to try to get hold of some poems to see if they contained any references to Rex. Was Maud Mandrake, née Kavanagh, the love of his life? For the first time she felt pity for her mother, hiding a broken heart under her slender black dress and lipsticked smile. But Daphne had obviously triumphed and the prize was debonair Rex who didn't like his son to use his name. It was inconceivable that her parents had remained together for her sake.

'I think your mother's poetry is awfully good,' she said as she brought in the coffee. They seemed to have got through two-thirds of a packet of chocolate wholemeal biscuits.

'Thanks.'

She didn't know if they were for the coffee or the compliment to his mother.

'But what were you doing in the woods? Were you looking for St Cloud?' He lost half a biscuit in his mug and had to search for it with his spoon.

'Dunno,' he mumbled. 'I did go there. I slept in the attic. I was scared. I was going to see him, about school and that, but then I thought he'd only send me back so I was going to live rough for a bit.'

'You mean you broke in?'

'I didn't take anything,' he said quickly. 'Only a bit of food. Where's my jacket?'

'In the kitchen – why?'

'I just wondered.'

So he had stolen something, and it was in his jacket. Money? A piece of silver?

'Were you hoping he might ask you to stay?'

'Mmm, I dunno. I mean, he wouldn't, would he?'

'I don't know,' she admitted.

'He never wanted me in the first place. He wanted my mother to get rid of me.'

'Oh, I'm sure he didn't.'

'He did. She spent the money on a dress – she told me.'

'She told you!'

'Mmm.'

'Oh Seamus, I'm sure the dress was just an excuse, I'm sure she really wanted you.'

'You don't know her,' he smiled affectionately.

'Oh dear, is that the time? I've got lots of things to do. Will you excuse me?' She hovered awkwardly. 'Would you like the television on? Or a book to read?'

'As long as it's not by Rex Beaumont.'

'Don't you like Daddy's books?'

'Well, the first one, *Silence*, I reckoned was really good but I don't go for those old murder and black magic stuff he writes now with his wife. I reckon he had one good book in him, and then he should've packed it in,' said his son, crossing the room to switch on the television.

'What about Daphne's books?' asked Daisy. 'How do you rate them?'

'I suppose they're all right if you like that sort of thing. I don't like the way they always end on a punch line. I mean, life goes on after the punch line, doesn't it?' Daisy tried to think of a punchy line to exit on.

'Of the three, I reckon Stanley's the best author,' he added.

'Stanley! Have you read him too? Have you met him? He hasn't published anything for years.'

'I met him once when I was little. He used to write to me sometimes, then he stopped. I expect it was because I never used to write back, but I used to like getting his letters.'

'It seems everybody knew but me,' said Daisy, exiting.

Rex would not have been surprised to learn that his son had read all his books, almost everybody had. Seamus had borrowed them one by one from the library and, hiding them lest they invoke Maud's wrath, had read them in secret in his camp bed behind the plywood partition, fingers in his ears to blot out sounds he did not wish to hear from his mother's room.

'Don't you want to watch "The Lady Vanishes"?' called Seamus, but the door had closed.

Daisy lay on Bryony's bed, absentmindedly hugging a teddy, her old bear, with her through all the changing scenes of life. He had even spent a short holiday in an abandoned station-master's house. So many questions: does your mother love my father, our father; does our father love your mother; does he make secret trips to see her, does my mother condone his visits? She heard again the obscene names Rex had called her when he burst in on her and Tom Greengrass when all the time he had a mistress and son stashed away in London. Maud Mandrake, of all people, that tasteless poetaster. 'Hypocrite! Hypocrite!' she told the bear, who regarded her with unchanged sad and glassy gaze.

She lay becalmed on the unmade bed. She saw now that she was stranded in time; while other people's lives went on, hers did not. Whatever there had been of her was no more. Her strength had been eroded. She was a zombie; the undead sliding inexorably into middle-age on a packet of detergent. How much time she had wasted.

She had been ill often as a child with bronchitis and spent long hours alone in bed with the radio. 'Housewife's Choice', 'Music While You Work', 'Five to Ten – A Story, A Hymn and a Prayer', 'Morning Story', twice daily 'Mrs Dale's Diary', 'the Archers'; these were her companions while the Lucozade lost its sparkle; it had stood by her bed all day. She ate tinned soup, brought in by Mrs Finch, to 'Midday Music Hall' and 'Workers' Playtime', the laughter in the works canteens echoing in her dusty bedroom. Robert Morton's Bumper Fun Book, Looby Loo, Ken Platt, and a comedian whose name she had forgotten who always finished his act by singing 'Life is just a Bowl of Cherries'.

Once, unexpectedly, Daphne came into her room, as if on cue, with a bowl of cherries, a smear of juice on her lip, for she had succumbed to temptation on the way up. It was Daisy's own yellow bowl with rabbits chasing each other's tails in a perpetual circle round the rim. Daphne picked out two pairs of twin cherries and hung them round her ears and twirled in front of the mirror, smiling at them nestling in her dark hair. Then she sat on the end of the bed and ate her glossy earrings.

'I wish I was pretty like you.'

'Not pretty, darling, that's such a wishy-washy word.'

It hurt Daisy to sit up and she lay back on her pillows.

'I'll read you a story.' Daphne took a book from the bookcase.

'Oh, *Little Women*. How I loved it! I used to know it by heart! "'Christmas won't be Christmas without presents,' grumbled Jo, lying on the rug."'

She was soon deep in the book, reading to herself, and Daisy fell asleep. When she woke in the sour afternoon she reached for a cherry and found only stones in the bowl.

Now her heart was thudding as she imagined Julian coming home and finding Seamus there. She knew he would think it was all her fault. She went downstairs.

'We must send a telegram to your mother at once. And the school. They may have contacted her and she may have gone home. People will be looking for you – maybe the police.'

'No!'

'We needn't say where you are. Just that you're O.K. I'm a mother myself. I know how she must be feeling.'

She pictured a distraught Maud running up and down Oxford Street into Soho clubs and pubs, thrusting a photograph of her son into the faces of indifferent teenagers.

'Give me the address please.'

'Oh, all right.'

As she dialled she saw Julian opening the next phone bill with charges for two telegrams.

'I bet your husband will be surprised when he comes home and finds me here.'

'I bet he will!'

The telephone rang. It was Daphne inviting Julian and Daisy to dinner. How odd. She thought she had said Stanley would be there but she was so flustered, as if Daphne could see Seamus sitting there, that when she put down the phone she couldn't remember when they were supposed to be going.

'Oh, Seamus, how dreadful of me, I've only just noticed you've got a bad cut on your head. It's because your hair's so red – why didn't you say? You must let me bathe it.'

'It's all right now. Watch the rest of the film – it's really good.'

'But Bryony will be home soon and I've done nothing.'

'It doesn't matter, does it? She won't mind.'

'I've just remembered, she's going out to tea. But I'm supposed to finish taking the tiles off the bathroom wall.'

'I'll help you.'

She sat down and they became engrossed in the film. When it finished Daisy shook herself back to reality and glanced round the room, appalled at the dirty mugs and biscuit crumbs. It looked almost as if people lived there.

As Seamus bent his head over the basin she felt an impulse to kiss the tender childish hollow of his neck, as she might have done Bryony's when she washed her hair. She steeled herself, over the reddened tufts of cotton-wool, to unveil an ignoble plan to him; that he might pass an unspecified number of nights in the summer house and spend the days with her.

'Don't you want your husband to know about me?'

'It's not that, it's just that I know he'd send you back at once and I'd like to keep you to myself for a little while.'

'What's his name?'

'Julian.'

'You're not scared of him, are you?'

'No, of course not, it's just that,' she admitted, 'he can be a bit of a bully.'

'How come you married him then?'

'Oh, I don't know, it's all so long ago. He wasn't always a bully. Something happened . . . it was such a relief at the time to meet someone who liked me. And someone who could go to the cinema and not analyse the film for hours afterwards and who'd never heard of Djuna Barnes and Gurdjieff and "Horizon" and things like that.'

'I've never heard of them,' said Seamus.

'Good. Would you mind if we made a start on those tiles?'

As they worked together, standing in the bath, she learned that Seamus was a member of the C.N.D. and had taken part in many marches and demonstrations; she almost envied him.

'I suppose I've become awfully wet,' she confessed. 'I used to have all sorts of principles and—'

'Not as wet as you will be,' said Seamus who was washing down the bath with the shower, spraying it at her.

Shrieking, laughing through the water, she grabbed it and directed its spray back at him until they and the bathroom were soaked. Blinded with water, they did not see an incredulous figure turn in the doorway and hurry away.

'This is a lovely house,' said Seamus, 'a real people's house.'

'What do you mean – real people?' asked Daisy, surprised.

'You know, the sort of people who have table mats and spare toothpaste and plasters in the bathroom cabinet, the sort of people who have a bathroom cabinet, like in the ads on television.'

'It's funny you should say that. When I was young I never thought we were real people. It's nice having a brother,' she added, looking away.

'How much does a place like this cost?'

'This one cost me my soul.'

'Do sit down, Seamus, you're making me nervous, pacing up and down like that. Are you bored? What would you like to do?'

'No. I'm not bored,' he lied at once.

His legs felt tired and irritable, he stretched them out. He could do with a good game of football; he thought back to his school in Islington, where he had been happy; his former friends.

'Don't you ever go out? Down the pub, or parties and that?'

'Of course we do, sometimes. No, not really. That is, Julian used to be in the Rugby Club and I used to help with the teas on Saturdays '

A painful memory clouded her face.

'What's wrong?'

'Oh! nothing.'

'Something I said?'

'No, I just remembered something but I can't tell you – it's too humiliating.'

'Go on, I won't mind.'

'I can't – it's too awful. Oh well, I might as well, I suppose. I once made some little quiches for the Rugby Club Supper and they started throwing them at each other.'

'Why?'

'They didn't like them.'

'I bet they were nice, really.'

'Everybody knew I'd made them. Julian cried in the "Gents". Then when he came out, he started throwing them too.'

There was a silence. Then Seamus asked, 'What are quiches?'

'I thought it might be an act of solidarity, showing them that we didn't care, but I wasn't really sure. I threw a spoonful of rice salad at someone, only it turned out to have been made by the Captain's wife and a horrible silence fell over the whole room. I was never asked to anything again. Not that I minded not going any more. I didn't like the other wives anyway, but I always seem to let Julian down. They're sort of tarts,' she added after a minute.

'They sound it.'

'Quiches, I mean.'

'What's he like, though, Julian?' he insisted. 'He seems a big bloke from what I've seen of him. Is he very posh or brainy or what?'

'There's less to him than meets the eye.'

They were frozen by the door chimes. The double note sounded again, imperatively.

'I'd better go,' said Daisy.

She came back, smiling with relief.

'It was only someone asking for jumble.'

'You know, you look really pretty when you laugh.'

'Then I must look hideous three-quarters of the time,' she snapped back, regretting her words as she spoke.

As soon as Daisy had said to Seamus that the house had cost her her soul she realised that it was not the truth, but she left the words on the air as she saw a bride and groom standing in front of a priest in ceremonial robes; they turned to face each other and the bride's face was a skull. The groom kissed her and she laid her white metacarpals on his sleeve and they turned and walked down the aisle. Of course she and Julian had not been married in a church, but she could remember almost nothing of the ceremony; it was a coloured blur, pierced with some violet-scented guilt concerned with Julian's mother. What were the solemn vows they had exchanged; what had she promised? She did not know. Did it mean that they were not married in the sight of God?'

■ CHAPTER NINE ■

'Stop picking at your food, Goliath.'

Geoffrey Cruikshank was forking helplessly through a pile of seaweed, which Maud had plucked from her native shore and boiled for their supper, as if hoping to uncover a tiny sea slug or shell that might excuse him from eating this delicacy. He had brought his gramophone into her room.

'Sorry,' he said, answering to the new pet-name that Maud had conferred on him when she returned from Ireland sooner than expected, disposed to be much friendlier than before, and winkled him out of his room like a whelk on a pin. She was eating hers with relish.

'Do you think we might have another record on?' she asked. 'Fond as I am of "The Laughing Policeman" . . .'

'Sorry.' He jumped up, managing to tip his seaweed in a steaming heap onto the floor.

'Oh, dear, now look what I've done . . .'

'Never mind,' cried Maud gaily, scooping it back onto the plate. 'The brine in it will kill any germs from the floor.'

The state of the floor reminded her of Seamus.

'I do miss him,' she sighed – to the strains of 'Happy Days are Here Again'.

'Who, John McCarron?'

'Seamus, you fool! Seamus, my only son. I don't want to hear that other's name mentioned.'

'Oh yes, of course. He never did get round to showing me his poetry.'

'What shall we do? Should we go to the police?'

'Well, the telegram did say he was all right . . .'

'Yes, but where is he? His father's no use, he couldn't care less that his only son is out somewhere in the wide, wide world with no one to look after him. He may have fallen into the wrong hands, someone may be holding him against his will . . .'

71

She drank deeply from her glass.

'It's difficult, bringing up a child on your own with no one to turn to. It's all Rex's fault – if he hadn't insisted on sending him to that stupid school. We were so happy here, just the two of us. And you, of course.'

'I thought you wanted him to go, so that you could have more freedom?' said Goliath innocently.

'Never!' cried Maud. 'Never. I let him think I wanted him to go because I thought it would be for the best for him. I even went off with that creature and let myself be humiliated over the length and breadth of Ireland so he would think I wanted him to go; I sacrificed myself on the altar of motherhood to give him a decent chance in life.'

'Don't cry, please don't cry.' He fished in his pocket and pulled out a red silk hanky followed by a blue one, a green one, a yellow one, a black one, a long string of conjuror's handkerchiefs.

'Sure, it would take more than these twenty silk hankies to dry my tears,' sobbed Maud, dabbing her eyes.

'I want to apologise. It seems that I have misjudged you.'

When she had said that she had been humiliated over the length and breadth of Ireland, Goliath pictured her small figure buffeted by the wind, toiling across a relief map of that country. He glanced down; the heels of her poor little boots were quite worn down. He touched one, shyly, with a finger.

'I know what you're thinking,' she wept, 'and I won't let you do it.' She started on the green hanky. 'I won't let you spend nearly forty pounds that you can ill-afford of your hard-earned money on a new pair of shoes for me!'

The sight of Seamus's football softly expiring in a corner provoked more tears.

The meal ended with Goliath kneeling beside her chair, begging to be allowed to buy her a new pair of shoes. A slight smile played at her mouth and was at once buried in a black handkerchief that hid all but her tragic eyes. Magic Carnival Novelties did not open the following morning, but it is doubtful that anyone noticed. After a late breakfast Maud and Goliath called in at the local police station on their way back from the shoe shop, but the desk sergeant was busy taking down particulars from someone claiming a lost dog and after five minutes Maud, raising her eyes to the ceiling, turned and clicked out in her new shoes, followed by Geoffrey.

▪ CHAPTER TEN ▪

The promised venison had failed to materialise. Julian told Daisy that she must manage without it. He had written out a menu and shopping list for her and she, in her preoccupation with Seamus, had mislaid them.

'Good grief,' she cried, right at the dénouement of 'General Hospital', which they were watching together. 'It's that ghastly dinner party tomorrow and I haven't even started to panic properly yet, or anything . . .' A great shuffling through cupboards and drawers ensued in the search for the missing menu. Seamus was horrified to see her transformed into a white-faced, wild-eyed mindless muttering thing with letters and papers fluttering through her distracted hands. He was restless, bored with being in the house, jumping every time the doorbell or telephone rang. He thought Surrey must be the most boring place on earth. He longed for Islington. He went over to the window, feeling himself in the way. It was raining; everything was dripping. Beyond the garden was a field where horses lounged about in mackintoshes. At last she found it, only to slump, head in hands, uttering dismal groans as she read Julian's small neat script. It seemed that the house must be cleaned from top to bottom and the entire garden tidied. As Seamus hoovered the master bedroom he caught sight of his reflections in a glass triptych and wondered what on earth he was doing there. He liked his new sister, even loved her, and did not want to hurt her but he knew he could not breathe the heavy air of Surrey any longer. He started to compose a farewell speech in which he stated that seeing Daisy's concern for her daughter had made him think of his own mother and how worried she must be. He sat down at the dressing-table and was absentmindedly dabbing a drop of cologne behind his ear when he heard the sound of a motor and saw a police car driving into the looking-glass.

Daisy ran upstairs, planning to tell Seamus that the police had come for him and to watch his face dissolve in relief when he realised it was a joke. They had come to warn her about a spate of robberies in the area. She found the hoover abandoned on the carpet, the air heady with the scent of cologne from the spilled bottle on the dressing-table and Seamus gone. She would not have thought he could leave a room so empty.

She did not dare to go out, although there was the shopping for tomorrow's dinner party, in case he should telephone, but wandered about the house from room to room. Then when Julian came home, she dreaded the telephone's ring. When Julian asked if she was all set for tomorrow, she lied that she was.

'Good! That means you'll have time to give the house a thorough going-over tomorrow and tidy up the front garden. I think I'll just run the mower over the grass. And for God's sake paint that gate early, so that it's dry before they arrive!'

Minutes later she heard him interrogating Bryony who was denying loudly any knowledge of a sleeping bag in the summer house. She went out.

'I put it there,' she said, her voice preceding her across green yards of grass.

'I will not tolerate lies,' Julian was saying.

'I put it there,' she repeated. She almost told him everything. His wrath could not make her misery any more acute, but she was so unused to telling him the truth about anything that she heard herself say, 'I was clearing out the cupboards and I put the sleeping bag out to air.'

'Why put it in the summer house?'

'It was raining.'

She thought Julian looked at her as if she was madder than he'd feared but he accepted the explanation. He threw it at Bryony. 'Put it away.' He turned to Daisy.

'You didn't clean out the grassbox properly last time you used this thing. I've had to waste ten minutes on it.'

'You go round this place snouting for trouble like a pig rooting for truffles,' she muttered.

'What?'

'Sorry, I thought I had cleaned it. Don't you think perhaps, the grass is a bit wet to cut?'

'If you've nothing better to do than stand around criticising me – oh God, what's she doing now?'

Bryony had put on the sleeping bag and was jumping across the lawn as if in a sack race. She fell over in her slippery blue sack and decided to roll the rest of the way. Daisy felt cheered; if Bryony dared to do that she had not yet been too blighted by the bitter marital air.

Later that night, if Julian had not been doing the same thing himself, he might have noticed that Daisy was giving a rather unconvincing performance of a sleeper. She lay huddled against the wall with her back to him, like a cow asleep in a field, a bitter, secondhand, balking cow which loomed in his path.

Daisy felt sorry for Julian, his chest rising and falling gently in his clean striped pyjamas, who would not tolerate lies and so was lied to all the time. She fell asleep, vowing to try harder and to make tomorrow's dinner party a real success and was pursued through dreamland by dishes and napkins and flowers and knives and forks and meat and puddings and garden forks and hoovers and dusters and shampoo and ironing boards.

▪ CHAPTER ELEVEN ▪

Rex had no qualms as he riffled through the books for sale on the window ledge of the library. It was unlikely that any of his works would be there; if, because of their popularity, they fell into disrepair they would be sent for rebinding and if, because a new edition had taken its place, one of them should be offered for sale, it would be snapped up at once. His first novel was now part of the A-level syllabus and Rex, with uncharacteristic reticence, had turned down recently an invitation to illuminate it for the sixth form of a local school. *Moonlight on Dunkirk*, its successor, was on the shelf; its label was satisfactorily studded with date stamps, but it had never achieved the critical or popular acclaim of *Silence*. Of Daphne's quartet of novels, only the first, *Fair Maids of February*, was there.The remainder were out at their task of provoking smiles through the tears of the citizens of Dorking.

Rex drifted over to the Literature section where, among the poetry, he picked out a faded copy of Stanley's anthology of decadent poetry *Pale Lost Lilies*. It had been borrowed only once in the last two years, an obvious candidate for withdrawal and sale at ten pence. It was typical of Stanley that it had appeared in the same week as a Penguin collection of *fin de siècle* verse. Rex stepped back in alarm and disbelief as he saw a book entitled *Silence*, by some Japanese author. He hurried over to Crime. He was reassured by the row of Max Maltravers Mysteries, by Rex and Daphne Beaumont, red stickers on their spines, with gaps in the ranks where volumes had been removed by discriminating borrowers. He pulled one out, *The Scarlet Pentangle*, and began to read. He became aware that he had been standing there for some time. He turned to a woman hovering beside him.

'I can recommend this one,' he smiled.

'Oh, have you read it?'

'I wrote it.'

Rex was able to provide a pen and a card on which to sign his autograph.

'Actually,' the woman said as he wrote, 'I think I like *Silence* the best of all your books.'

The pen splattered, disfiguring the card with an ugly blot.

The Max Maltravers weren't bad; Rex thought that his contribution anyway deserved one reviewer's comment that not only were they mirrors of contemporary life but also rattling good yarns; but they weren't good enough. Perhaps he should make his autobiography his magnum opus. After all he had led an interesting life. The thought of Seamus rose like another blot, a full stop. He could go up as far as the army; do his childhood, poignant portraits of his parents, a golden idyll; first pangs of love in the watermeadows of Winchester; Cambridge, omitting the fact that he had had the distinction of being ignored by the greatest don of his day; his service in the war; the whole narrative studded with brilliant names like a winter sky of stars. He saw a poster advertising its serialisation in a Sunday newspaper; chat shows, queues of buyers holding out glossy books for signature. His wrist buzzed in anticipation.

On his way out he picked up a couple of bargains. The doomed authors smiled painfully from their dustjackets. He held the door for a frail octogenarian, feeling a pang that she would not be able to hang on long enough to read his masterwork. He winced as she planted her walking frame on his foot.

He limped into Meadowbank, a little recreation ground, and lit a cigarette and watched the ducks on the lake. The wind blew the smoke into his eyes, the red cone burned fiercely down the white tube, the expensive paper crackled. A truant boy, or perhaps one convalescing from an illness, was flying a kite. He held a handle in each hand, making a red aeroplane swoop and swirl and loop the loop, dancing on its twin wires, dazzling in the sunshine. As Rex watched, an idea for the perfect murder came to him. A beautiful girl lies dead on a lonely beach. There is no sound but the suck of the sea and the cries of the gulls. There are no footprints but hers on the wet sand. Far off, on a cliff or in a lighthouse, the murderer reels in his kite and puts away his wires, as dispassionate as a grocer after cutting a slice of cheese.

'One advantage of not having Public Lending Right,' Rex told Daphne at home that evening, 'is that one can read the books of authors one despises without putting a penny in their pockets.'

'You'd think that at least one of them might have telephoned,' she replied.

'Perhaps they got the date wrong?'

'It's just common courtesy.'

'Well, anyway, we can enjoy it. I'm starving.'

'We can't. It's dried to a frazzle. Ruined.' Daphne stared tragically at her wrecked dinner.

'Get your coat. I'll take you out to eat. By the way, I've got the plot for Max's next.'

Mrs Finch would be supping on the burned remnants of the meal she had spent the afternoon preparing.

'If it wasn't so undignified,' Daphne went on, as she swung her legs into the car, 'I'd go round and confront them with their defection. I might have expected it of Stanley, but not Daisy!'

'What do you fancy, Indian, Chinese, Italian, Spanish?'

'I don't care. Come to think of it, she was very offhand on the phone.'

Rex parked outside La Golondrina.

'Doesn't look very salubrious.' He hesitated on the pavement.

'Oh, never mind! Let's go in.' Daphne pushed open the door; the wind bellied her thin silver cloak.

They were met by a gust of warm pungent air and jovial laughter.

'It's old Rex, and Daphne! Come in and join us.'

Two tables had been pushed together down the centre of the small restaurant. At the head, dressed as a Roman centurion, sat Jasper Corrigan, an actor whom they knew slightly. On his right was a girl with long fair hair who seemed to be weeping into a paper napkin. He jumped up and embraced them, then snatched a couple of chairs from the side table where two diners cowered, the candle-light striking the golden fleece on his great arms and thighs. His entourage was forced to shift its chairs to accommodate Rex and Daphne; there was much grumbling at the lower end of the table. The *padrone* mopped and mowed, beaming as if all he had needed to make his happiness complete was to have his door blocked by brawny theatricals.

'We've been filming in your neck of the woods,' Jasper told them. 'At the chalkpits. Marvellous scenery.'

'We like it,' said Daphne rather coldly, not liking the thought of this mob scrambling about over the white chalk and scaring the blue butterflies out of the rock roses and little pink and blue and white and purple milkworts that grew there.

'Thank you,' as he poured her some wine from one of the several bottles on the table.

'Are you in the film?' Rex turned to the girl on his right who was obviously making an effort to pull herself together and was crumbling a piece of roll in her mouth, her pink eyes testifying to whatever it was that troubled her. She raised them to him, chewing fast so that she could answer. Before she had finished her dry mouthful, Jasper was saying loudly in a sudden silence that had fallen over the table. 'She's just some sort of menial who runs around with a clapper board, getting in everybody's way.'

This produced a fresh flood. Somebody who did not know Daphne better might have thought it was sympathy for the girl's plight that made her lean across the table and engage her in conversation. Rex was not deceived. He saw how Daphne could not resist a flickering comparison of her own white beringed hand, tipped with exquisite pink nails, and the poor, stubby, bitten-nailed paw on which she laid it. She managed to bring a wan smile to the girl's face. She even popped a prawn from its green bed on her plate onto the girl's and prevailed on her to eat it.

The actor's bloodshot eyes narrowed as the pink crustacean vanished down the red lane. His fingers tightened on a roll, crushing it, he picked it up, looked at Daphne, hesitated, then flung it with full force at one of two bit players engaged in a private joke at the opposite end of the table. After a moment's surprise, during which the target pulled crumbs from his beard, the air was filled with flying missiles. The table divided into two warring factions; those seated in the middle hurled rolls and breadsticks indiscriminately to either side. The tearful continuity girl was hit in the eye, then she took the opportunity to dash a glass of wine into Jasper's face. He leaped to his feet, roaring like a wounded beast and shook the table with both hands so that wine and water spilled and knives and forks jumped and danced. The *padrone* ran in to watch the fun. How he laughed. Then he was hit by a prawn.

'Oh! good shot!' he moaned. Jasper Corrigan's good humour was restored instantly. The bombardment stopped as suddenly as it had started.

'Carlos,' he said, 'I don't know how you expect your guests to eat in a mess. Get someone to clear it up.' He waved his arm grandly at the debris. 'At once!'

'Right away, sir,' he beamed.

He summoned a skinny little fellow in a stained white coat and checked cook's trousers, with a brush and dustpan. Daphne had to smile at the way his chef's hat, which was absurdly big, made his ears stick out. As he swept, his hat tilted over his glasses and he knelt up to right it, looking straight into Daphne's amused gaze.

'Stanley!'

He stared at her for a moment, then went on with his sweeping.

'Rex! Take me home!'

Rex placed some money on the table and took Daphne's cloak from the hatstand and draped it round her shoulders. The silver cloak had been hit by a flying dollop of sauce and as Daphne walked out she looked as if she had been shot in the back.

▪ CHAPTER TWELVE ▪

Was there no one to shout 'Kong's loose!' or 'The dam's burst,' or 'The Martians have landed,' no catastrophe to rescue her from this dreadful day? Only the Surrey landscape, only a leading cow drawing the undulating black and white silk ribbon of the herd past a hedge, only a bee pretending it was a day such as any other when one might as well rub one's velvety back in a freckled foxglove, only a wasp kicking wildly in the milk jug, its heavy wings pulling it down into a white death. Daisy rescued it with a spoon; it crawled up the handle onto her finger and stung her. Ordinarily she might have been pleased; it was not often that something so exciting happened to her; but today she could do without a finger that was showing signs of metamorphosing into a sausage. Perhaps she was one of those people who were allergic to stings? Could she phone Julian and tell him to cancel the dinner and rush off to Casualty? No hope there; although her finger was flashing red and white alternately like a beacon or distress signal, she had to admit that she felt perfectly all right. Things to do, things to do! Perhaps a list of them would save her. She got a pencil and paper – shopping, cooking, wash hair, iron dress – and then she fell to drawing. A cup of coffee to stimulate her to wash her hair, then housework while it dried, then catch the bus. Why this panic seeping like poisonous gas through the floor, rising and choking her? She tried to imagine circumstances in which this day would seem Heaven on earth; a prison, hospital. Hospital! She looked at a puff of steam blown from the kettle's spout. She looked at her hand. She carried the kettle to the sink. She poised it above her outstretched hand. She put it down. The surgery would be closed. She would have to ring the doctor at home or get somebody to drive her to the hospital. She pictured herself presenting a huge white bandaged mitt to Julian. Letting him down again. She saw herself, pale and dull; the Cluff-Trenches inserting her disastrous food between yawns. How did one have a nervous breakdown? Was it imperative to take off one's clothes and run down the street, or could one just go into the local shop and knock down pyramids of tins and scream until an injection in the arm granted merciful silence and a pleasantly somnolent ride in an ambulance to a destination unknown? If not, how would anyone know one had had a nervous breakdown? But Bryony. It wasn't worth it. Tomorrow today will be yesterday. What on earth's so terrible about entertaining your husband's boss and his wife to a meal? Surely even you are capable of that. Get upstairs and wash your hair – which you should have done last night. Julian's right about you. The new tiles, Julian's handiwork, gleamed prettily on the bathroom wall. Dimly, through a curtain of dripping hair, came the sub-aquatic shrilling of the telephone.

'It's the school here. Bryony's had a bit of a fall from the apparatus. We took her to the surgery and Doctor had a look at her and said she has no signs of concussion, but he thinks she should take things quietly for the rest of the day so Mrs Marshall is bringing her home in the car.'

Bryony had been placed on the back seat. She sat up, pale, with a bruise over her eye and a sheepish grin, as Daisy rushed to open the door. As she embraced her, pity for the bruised forehead, relief that it wasn't worse, and guilt that her prayer for deliverance had been answered in such a way flooded through Daisy. Bryony placed a small hand in unconscious absolution on her mother's wet head. Daisy carried her to a sofa and turned to thank Mrs Marshall. As the teacher drove away, Daisy realised that the zip of her jeans had slipped down. Bryony sprang back from the looking glass on the wall where she was studying her face as her mother re-entered the room.

'I hope I get a black eye,' she said. Daisy moaned slightly at the thought of green and purple tinging that soft brow. When Bryony was settled with the cat, a drink, books, a teddy and a pre-school programme on the television, Daisy went to ring Julian.

'Mummy,' came Bryony's voice as she picked up the receiver. 'What happened to that soldier in the wood who was crying?'

'I – I don't know.'

'I wonder where he is now?'

'Yes. I wonder.'

'Well. She's all right, isn't she?'

'Well, the doctor thought she might be a little concussed.' She crossed her fingers.

'There's obviously no reason to cancel tonight. You're just using it as an excuse.'

His voice hissed through the receiver; he was obviously afraid of being overheard. Venom sizzled in the little holes.

'But I won't be able to do any shopping!' she wailed.

'You told me you'd done it all! You can spend some time in the garden. Get Bryony to give you a hand.'

His voice changed. Someone had obviously come into the room.

'Don't worry, darling. I'll be home as soon as I can. Give Bryony a kiss from me.'

He put down the telephone.

As the Cluff-Trenches cruised along between hedges high with cowparsley, poppies and mallow, he preoccupied with a letter to the Council protesting about the hazards to motorists of these unkempt weeds, and her large face heavy with its own thoughts of the baby-sitter rifling through her silken underwear, they had no idea of the turmoil at Fairlawn, in anticipation of their dread wheels in the drive.

'There's a dead moth in this light!'

'Never mind! They won't be coming into the kitchen!'

'They might!'

Julian was on the kitchen stool disengaging the cover of the fluorescent tube.

'Is Bryony's room tidy?'

'No more than usual.'

'Well, for God's sake tidy it! They once made me gaze on a sleeping infant!'

'That was a new baby.'

Julian jumped down and came at her with a duster. She fled. When she returned he was attacking the sink with a rubber plunger.

'Don't want a blockage, tonight of all nights.'

'Julian, you're just being neurotic. Go and sit down and have a drink!' She laid a tentative hand on his arm; he shrugged it off.

'Couldn't you have had the foresight not to cook chips for Bryony's tea tonight of all nights? The whole house reeks of fried fat!' He seized an aerosol and they were wreathed in circles of its scent as the telephone rang.

'It's them! They're cancelling! You get it.'

Julian stood paralysed. Daisy ran to the telephone, blessing the

Cluff-Trenches for having the grace to excuse them from this nightmare. 'Hello,' she said, heart thudding, fingers crossed. There followed rapid pips, then the sound of a coin pushed into a call-box; then the harsh drilling noise of lost money. Seamus. She knew at once. Was he safe, was he in trouble? Had he lost his last few pence trying to call her? She put down the receiver and stood for a minute or two, waiting for the phone to ring again.

'Well?' Julian stood in the doorway.

'Wrong number.'

'Are you sure?' he asked suspiciously.

'Of course I'm sure.' Don't let him ring again now, let him ring tomorrow and tell me he's all right.

'I'll just run the carpet sweeper over the hall carpet. You go and get changed.'

'I am changed.'

They were stabbed by the front-door chimes.

'You look pathetic,' said Julian and walked smiling to open the door. He winced as Jeanne Cluff-Trench's hand hovered over the finger plate on the lounge door.

'Put your fingers on the finger plates if you want to,' he assured her jovially. 'Only takes a spot of Brasso to shine them up again.' She looked surprised but, thinking to grant his odd request, obliged with two pudgy smears.

'Good, lovely!' laughed Julian. 'Just the job,' adding a set of his own prints. 'Come on in—take a pew. What would you like to drink? You've met my wife, haven't you? She hasn't had time to change. She's the casual type. Doesn't stand on ceremony. Get the Brasso,' he hissed at her.

'Couldn't we have a little more light?' asked Julian, as they sat down in the dining room.

'Mehr Licht,' said Daisy. It was essential that the meal be conducted in as little light as possible.

'Oh I think the candles are lovely. Such a nice soft light!' Jeanne Cluff-Trench came to her rescue, then threatened to engulf them all in darkness with her perfumed breath. The flames faltered and recovered their poise.

'Some people think Goethe's last words were *"Mehr Licht"* but actually he is supposed to have said, *"Macht doch den zweiten Fensterladern auch auf, damit mehr Licht hereinkomme!"* I used to think they were some eminent Scot's dying words; Scott or Burns or Barrie at the Auld Licht Kirk, "Mair licht", if you see what I mean,' Daisy was telling Giles Cluff-Trench, who was looking at her rather strangely. Obviously it had not been a good idea to sneak those extra drinks in the kitchen in the hope of adding sparkle to her conversation.

'Aren't we going to eat?' asked Julian coldly.

'Of course. I'm sorry.'

She took a tray of four little dishes from the sideboard and placed one before each person.

'This is delicious! What is it?'

'It's a sort of fish mousse.'

'Mmm – lovely. You must give me the recipe.'

As if on cue, the cat came into the room, tail in the air, mewing loudly, as if enquiring what had become of his dinner. Daisy excused herself and took him up to Bryony's room. She was tempted to climb into the bed and lie down beside her and sleep until the guests were gone. She envied the cat, who was doing that.

'Are you going away this summer?' Julian and Jeanne Cluff-Trench were asking each other, in unison, when she returned.

They all laughed.

'Ladies first,' smiled Julian.

'Well, we went to the Seychelles at Easter, as you know, which was absolutely gorgeous, so it's down to Devon this summer, I'm afraid. How about you?'

'Devon.' Julian grimaced at the golden beaches and green cliffs. Although it seemed that it was incumbent on them to go somewhere, there had seemed no point in paying to transport this unhappy little family to anywhere more prestigious.

'I like Devon!' asserted Giles Cluff-Trench.

'Oh, so do we.'

'Of course, with three sets of school fees, we're drawing in our horns a bit, aren't we, darling?' said his wife.

He was drawing in his knee, which had vainly sought Daisy's.

'Where does your little one go? She's a girl, isn't she?'

'Sometimes I wonder,' said Julian.

'She goes to the village school.'

'For the moment,' put in Julian quickly. 'We're looking around for a good school for her.'

'The village school's very good and she's very happy there,' said Daisy, staring at him in alarm at this fresh threat.

'Some of these village schools *are* good, up to a point,' conceded Jeanne Cluff-Trench, 'but our three are inclined to be academic and I do think you've got to give them the best possible chance, even if it does mean scrimping on things like holidays.'

'Do you know Seaton?' Giles Cluff-Trench demanded of Daisy.

'Seaton?'

'Seaton in Devon.'

'No, I'm afraid I don't, but it's supposed to be awfully nice I've heard. Why, have you been there?'

'No. I just wondered.'

'Drop more Valpollicella, anyone?'

Julian refilled the glasses.

He felt that he had lost face badly in admitting to a daughter at the village school and a holiday in Devon.

'This ratatouille's lovely,' enthused Jeanne Cluff-Trench, then added suspiciously, 'You're not vegetarians, are you? Oh! no, of course not – the fish mousse.'

'I was promised venison,' grumbled her husband.

'Chap who was getting it for me failed to produce the goods,' apologised Julian.

'We'd prefer to go abroad somewhere this holiday,' he blundered on, 'but we have to be a bit careful. Daisy's got a very sensitive skin. Burns easily. She got very badly burned on our honeymoon in Italy. We may change our minds and pick on somewhere a bit more exotic.'

Daisy's flaming cheeks seemed to bear out his lie. Their Italian honeymoon. The oleanders on the autostrada, those three dead dogs who must have been thrown from a car; the windscreen bleared with the blood of insects; lighted by fireflies to the gabinetti; what a waste, what a nonsense she and Julian had made of Italy.

'Penny for them?'

'I'm sorry. What did you say?'

'You were miles away.'

'I was thinking about the fireflies at Fiesole.'

'Your skin doesn't look as if it would burn. Excuse me, you don't mind, do you, Julian?'

Giles Cluff-Trench reached over and laid his hand on her cheek. No one else seemed to find it odd that he should ask Julian's permission to touch Daisy's face.

'No. I'm surprised that you should burn. Let me see your arm.' He examined it and turned it over.

'You've got quite a tan!' he said triumphantly.

'Skin types can change with time,' she said, withdrawing her arm. Julian had not seen those dead dogs, although they had sprawled, hugely dead at the side of the autostrada. Or perhaps he had.

'Your garden's lovely,' said Jeanne Cluff-Trench. 'Who does it?'

'I do,' they answered together.

'I mean, Julian does most of it,' said Daisy quickly.

'I do all the spade work,' laughed Julian, 'and she potters around with the secateurs.'

'We've just had ours re-landscaped.'

'I love going round garden centres on a Sunday morning, don't you?' asked Jeanne brightly. 'Have you been to Syon Park?'

'No,' answered Daisy, equally brightly. 'Have you?'

'No. But I'd love to go. In the springtime when the daffodils are in bloom. Lovely.'

'Lovely,' echoed Daisy. She saw the banks of daffodils running down to the river. She felt sure as she rose to bring in the pudding that neither of them would breathe the scent of those golden trumpets, let alone visit the house. She stayed as long as she dared in the kitchen, staring at the pudding in the cut-glass bowl as if by wishing she could transform it from strawberry flavoured Instant Whip, marbled with tinned strawberries and decked with blobs of Dream Topping, into the exquisite Strawberry Fool for which she hoped her guests would mistake it.

'More ratatouille, anyone?' Julian was asking with hopeless optimism as she re-entered. 'There is some left, isn't there, Daisy?'

'There's another – I mean, yes, there is some left.'

Nobody wanted any.

'How do you get such a smooth texture?' Jeanne Cluff-Trench was asking, but Daisy was saved from replying by the front-door chimes. She and Julian stared at each other, then, 'I'll get it,' he said, as if it was quite usual for someone to call on them in the evening.

Then it seemed as if he was blown back into the room by a small tornado mouthing silently against the wind. Daisy saw her mother-in-law, with a suitcase in one hand and a cardboard box in the other, then Bryony came hurtling down the stairs and almost swept her off her feet, flinging herself on her.

'Nanny!'

'It's my wife's old nanny,' Julian explained, as his mother disengaged herself from Bryony's arms, and sidestepped from her embrace.

'You should have let us know you were coming, Nanny,' he said loudly, with the emphasis on the last word.

'Well,' she said, drawing up a chair. 'Well, I said to myself, if the mountain won't come to Mohammed, or perhaps it should be the other way round,' she chuckled, as she eased her shoes off her plump feet. 'That's better. Relief.' She wriggled her toes. Bryony climbed onto her knee. The Cluff-Trenches sat. Julian saw that Bryony was wearing a pair of beloved pyjamas which had been shorn off above the knee when the legs wore out.

'Would you like something to eat?' Daisy was asking.

'I'll just have a bit of that Instant Whip, duck, if there's any going spare.' The nightmare was complete. The Cluff-Trenches both raised their spoons to their mouths as if to put her words to the test. Julian pulled Bryony roughly from her grandmother's knee. 'Get off to bed now, dear. It's late.'

'Oh, she can stop up a bit longer,' chuckled Nan in her easygoing way. 'Have a look in that box, duck, I've brought you a present.'

Bryony knelt down and tore off the string. She put her hand in. There was a rustling sound. Her fingers felt something cold and hard like an Easter egg. She pulled it out. A little beaded reptilian head with bright blinking eyes, a dusty gold shell, a pointed tail, four little legs, making swimming motions in the air. She shrieked with delight. Jeanne Cluff-Trench shrieked in horror. Daisy fell on her knees beside Bryony to adore the shelly newcomer.

'Oh, he's lovely!' cried Bryony. 'Thank you Nana! Is he a boy or a girl? Oh! he hissed when I kissed him. He's lovely! What shall I call him? Look at his little nose! Oh, he's put his head in!'

'He's a bit bewildered, duck, seeing all these strange people in a strange country. He's a bit shy. He'll be all right when he comes out of his shell.'

'I'm not having that thing crawling around the garden,' Julian said. 'Daddy!'

'If it gets into the blades of the mower it will smash them to pieces.'

'Got a Flymo, have you?' asked Giles Cluff-Trench.

'No, actually. Although I'm thinking of getting one. Good, are they? Have you got one?'

'No, not really.'

Julian's mother was explaining to Jeanne Cluff-Trench, between spoonsful of pudding, how she had acquired the tortoise, who was now being introduced to the cat, who had come to join the party.

'Look, Blacky, it's your brother!'

'All by hisself in a tin bath he was, no grass nor nothing. Well, I couldn't just leave him there, could I?'

'I don't know,' said Jeanne faintly.

'It's a cruel trade, I said. "Don't give me that," he said. Yes, I said, downright cruel and I've got a good mind to report you. "Tell you what," he says, "seeing as it's closing time, you can have him for a nicker." So here we are.'

'She has got other pyjamas,' Daisy felt it incumbent on her to explain to the room at large, 'only those are her favourites and she won't let me throw them out.'

'They're my best ones,' said Bryony.

'Cheese and biscuits, anyone?' asked Julian miserably, glaring at his mother. 'Perhaps you'd like to freshen up?' He was feeling ashamed of his denial of her but there was nothing he could do now, which increased his anger with her.

'No, I'm fine thanks, lovey.'

'Not for me, thanks.'

'Nor me, couldn't eat another thing.'

Mrs Almond senior caught sight for the first time of the bruises above Bryony's eye. 'Whatever have you been doing to yourself? It wasn't . . . your Dad didn't . . .?' She was unable to formulate the accusation.

'I fell off the apparatus.'

'Oh! Well, that's all right then. He had a terrible temper as a boy,' she explained to the Cluff-Trenches, 'really evil. I remember once he . . .'

'Oh! Did you know him then? I'd no idea you two were childhood sweethearts, Daisy.'

'Yes.' 'No.' said Daisy and Julian.

'Know him? I ought to have!' laughed Mrs Almond comfortably, 'seeing as he's . . .'

'Nanny was friendly with my nanny,' explained Julian before she could finish.

'Don't shout, Julian – really, we're none of us deaf,' said his mother sharply, realising at last his perfidy.

'I was saying I ought to have known him—' she broke off.

'Have you put some arnica on that bruise?' She turned to Daisy.

'Yes.'

'What's arnica?' asked Bryony.

'That stuff I put on your bruise,' said Daisy desperately.

'Oh, I thought it was just water.'

'Get to bed, Bryony. You've got school tomorrow.'

Giles Cluff-Trench gave vent to a cough.

'That's a nasty cough you've got,' said Nanny. 'Are you taking something for it?'

'No, well, it's nothing really; at least so my wife tells me.'

'It doesn't do to neglect a cough,' Nanny told Jeanne sternly. 'You want to get him some of that whatsisname, like on the telly. You know, the one where the little girl comes down with a tickly cough and her Mum tells her, "the little French boy's coming tomorrow", though you'd think she'd have told her before – '

'Perhaps she wanted it to be a surprise,' suggested Bryony.

'I expect so, pet. Anyway, blow me, if the little French boy doesn't come down with a chesty cough hisself and her Mum tells him, or was it the tickly cough he got?'

'Jean-Pierre,' said Bryony.

'That's right, pet. She knows, you know.' She turned to the Cluff-Trenches for confirmation of her grand daughter's cleverness.

'Anyway, she tells him, "Jean-Pierre, in England when we get a cough, we take something or other" – I can't recall the name but it must be good. You want to get a bottle of that.'

Bryony felt her father's pincers on her arm.

'O.K., O.K., I'm going. I know when I'm not wanted.'

She gathered up her cat and tortoise in its box and staggered to the door.

'Good night, Mummy. Good night, everybody.'

'N'night, duck. God bless.'

'N'night, Nan.'

Daisy broke into silent tears. She remembered reading in the 'In Memoriam' column in the local paper: 'N'night Nan, God Bless.' The betrayed grandmother was describing to Jeanne Cluff-Trench her career as a 'Lollipop Lady'. Daisy went to get the coffee.

'There's something wrong here, I thought to myself, looking after other people's kids all day, when I've got one of my own that

I never see so, at four o'clock I stood my lollipop in the hall, changed out of my white mac, got a friend to take over for a few days, flung a few things into a suitcase, and here I am.'

It dawned on Giles Cluff-Trench that this woman was not Daisy's old nanny at all, but her mother. She certainly wasn't his idea of a famous writer. He didn't care much for being deceived, especially by his staff. He took out a small cigar and lit it; he didn't offer one to Julian, on whom this slight was not lost and to whom the blue smoke came as from the fires of hell. His mother reached for the cigar case.

'Mind if I try one? I've always wanted to smoke a cigar.'

'Be my guest.'

'Ta!'

She leaned forward and lit it in the candle and leaned back, eyes closed in ecstasy.

'Beautiful aroma – quite mild really. For the time of year,' she added by mistake.

Then she coughed and spluttered, expelling it from her mouth onto a plate, where she ground it out.

Giles Cluff-Trench ground his teeth. Jeanne Cluff-Trench looked grumpy.

'I suppose you haven't any cigarettes?' she asked Julian.

'I always keep a couple of packs for guests,' he answered triumphantly, rising and pulling out the sideboard drawer, then a frantic riffling ensued.

'I know they're here somewhere,' he said desperately, as napkins, napkin rings, table mats, a tray cloth and a set of mats embroidered and crocheted by his mother flew to the floor.

'Have you moved them?' he accused Daisy.

'Perhaps the, uh, you know, those friends who dropped in, smoked them all?'

A vain bid to save her own skin and Julian's face.

'Our local shop was out of menthol cigarettes, which are all she'll normally smoke, and the pub we stopped at didn't have any,' Giles Cluff-Trench explained to Daisy.

'No wonder she's feeling dis-Consulate.' She sympathised.

'Let's go into the lounge for coffee and liqueurs,' said Julian faintly, hoping his mother would linger and he could find some pretext for getting rid of her, perhaps lock her in the kitchen. She led the way.

'What will you have? Brandy, Drambuie, Cassis, Crème-de-Menthe, Tia Maria? I think I've got just about anything you care to mention.'

He had had, until Seamus had been moved to sample the jewelled liquids on the sideboard.

'Cassis for me, please.'

'I'll just have a brandy.'

'I'll get them,' said Daisy quickly. 'What will you have, Julian?'

'I'll keep Giles company.'

'I'll have a drop of brandy too if it's not too strong,' said his mother.

The brandy was no problem, but Cassis! The bottle was empty. 'Excuse me a minute,' she went to the kitchen where she looked round desperately for something purple. Methylated spirit? No. Ah, Ribena! She half-filled the little glass and added a measure of gin. Then, in the unlikely case of more being requested, mixed up more of the formula in the Cassis bottle and carried them through on a tray, with a silver dish of extra-strong peppermints.

Scarce had the coffee scalded their lips when the front-door chimes sent cups rattling in saucers.

'Who the hell?' began Julian. Daisy was already rising to answer it. The figure of a boy was outlined in the bower of honeysuckle over the porch, moths flocked into the light. How sweet and soft the night air was, the moon high in a milky penumbra above opalescent clouds. If he had taken her hand she would have walked out into the dewy garden with him.

'Have you any jumble?' he asked, having remembered that someone had once called at the house with that request.

'Oh Seamus!'

Giddy with wine she stepped forward and almost fell on him.

'I'm collecting on behalf of the Scouts. You wouldn't have any old battledress jackets, would you?'

'I'll get it!'

She ran in and dragged his jacket out of the cupboard under the stairs where she had bundled it. As she did so an envelope of folded papers fell to the floor. Julian was coming. She shut the cupboard and took the jacket and thrust it at Seamus.

'Who is it?' called Julian.

'Just a boy, collecting jumble. See you in the morning?' she whispered, closing the door.

'What an odd time to be collecting jumble,' commented Jeanne. 'What are some parents thinking of?'

'It was for the Scouts,' explained Daisy.

Giles Cluff-Trench went to the bathroom. Julian, on the pretext of showing him where it was, managed to dart in first to check that all was well with the new tiles and give the air a cautionary squirt of freshener.

When he rejoined the ladies, his mother was describing various jumble sales she had attended over the years, and emerged as something of an expert in the strategy and tactics thereof.

'I picked up a marvellous school pullover for 10p'—Jeanne Cluff-Trench attempted to compete—'perfect condition!'

'Well, I bought Bryony a school jumper in Marks two years ago and it's been marvellous, it still fits. It seems to grow with her somehow and comes up like new when it's washed—I'm not sure what it cost but it's been worth—'

'I'm sure nobody wants to hear about Bryony's school pullover,' put in Julian heavily. After that no one had anything much to say and the Cluff-Trenches had another drink, in silence, and then rose to go, thanking them for a lovely evening.

'I've seen one of your books in the library,' said Giles Cluff-Trench cryptically to Nanny as he left. He bent over Daisy's hand and kissed it. Nanny was still puzzling over what he had meant as she searched the larder, in vain, for Ovaltine.

When she had seen her mother-in-law settled in her room she gazed for a few moments on her sleeping daughter, Blacky snored gently, silence from the tortoise box, and Daisy stole back downstairs to the cupboard and picked up the papers which had fallen from Seamus's jacket. She switched on the light and stood among the brushes and hoover and dusters staring at it. Surely it was Stanley's writing, but it was not a letter. She read: 'I thought silence was just absence of noise. I didn't know that silence had pillars and porticoes, corridors stretching endlessly, labyrinths; silence grows like mould, like frost . . .'

She sank onto a pair of wellingtons which crumpled beneath her. It was the opening paragraph of Rex's great success, on brittle yellow paper, in Stanley's handwriting—with Stanley's name on the title page.

'It can't be . . .' she whispered as she stowed the sheets under a box of polishes. 'It can't be. Daddy?'

As at the end of every day, no matter what had passed within it, the bed lay berthed in the dim light of the bedroom waiting to carry the sleepers through whatever seas they must sail, and then return them, bumping gently on the shore of morning. Daisy pulled the quilt over her and gave herself to darkness, wishing that she might never wake to morning and its reckoning. She remembered that the sleeping bag was no longer in the summer house as sleep clamped an iron helmet over her head and she turned from some faint accusation, to the wall.

An hour later she woke from a dream of school. Her heart was beating painfully and irregularly. It frightened her. She longed for a drink of water but dared not leave the bed for fear of waking Julian. The dinner party, in garish colours, was replayed against the backcloth of the darkness; greasy lips, harsh caws of laughter, terrible black silences, Julian's mother's arrival on her little bowed legs, the melancholy reptile's on his; Julian's betrayal of his mother, her own acquiescence in it; her gaucheness. Her face hovered over the table like a balloon with bloody mascara and clownish patches of red on the cheeks and, as she lay in bed, burned in memory. She felt strangled by the duvet, suffocated by the heavy curtains, felt Julian draining the oxygen from the air and black carbon dioxide swirling round the room. A green circle of numbers floated at the bedside; two slender luminous hands rested on the figure one and a nervous gnomon flickered through the seconds of her life. If only, she thought, I could put back the clock. Or rather, the calendar.

Such a trite wish, expressed at that moment no doubt by millions of people all over the world, but no less agonisingly true for that. 'The moving finger writes . . .' How she had hated those lines at school, suspecting them of cliché even then, and now she was lying watching a moving finger inscribing them in chalk on a blackboard (Miss Windibank had insisted on calling it the greenboard, because it was). Absurd, she thought, drying her ear where the tears had gathered in a pool, with the corner of the duvet, to be wishing herself back at school, but school was where she had destroyed her life and several other peoples' lives. There were two things she could not comprehend now, years later: why had she not killed herself then—it was too late now because of Bryony—and her incredible naivete in believing him when he had told her everything was over between him and his wife and that she did not care what he did.

The art room was a prefabricated hut stuck like an afterthought beyond the canteen, reached by stepping stones set in the rough grass which were flooded frequently, so that mud mingled with spilled powder paint on the floor. Drawing her first breath there, Daisy was intoxicated by its smell, a blend of French tobacco and linseed oil, turpentine and paper and paint and clay, and the elusive woody scent of the brittle tutus of pencil shavings frilled with colour that fell from the big cranky sharpener clamped to the desk and broke on the floor.

Mr Greengrass and his subject were not regarded highly by the rest of the staff. He wore jeans and faded corduroy jackets; when occasion demanded that he wore one, a school tie knotted insolently under the open collar of his shirt. He was tall, with a lock of brown hair that had to be pushed back from his narrow face with stained fingers when he stooped over the girls' work. He smoked Gauloises, which he stubbed in the lids of coffee jars when another member of staff was seen picking her way over the stepping stones to the annexe. Although disliked and feared for his sarcasm by most of the girls, he was popular with the less law-abiding members of the community for his obvious scorn for school rules and discipline; he had been seen drinking from a small bottle on Sports Day. Later, a girl had fallen in the relay and risen from the turf with a circle of blood on her knee, where she had fallen on the bottle top. It had cost her the race.

Daisy worked quietly and painstakingly at a desk, in the centre of the room, which the teacher in his pacings did not often visit. It was on the drawing boards of those fortunates at the back and front of the class that his ash fell and left charcoal-like smudges and at the end of the lesson, when the others handed in their work, hers was scrumpled surreptitiously into the waste bin and she was left with a deflated feeling of disappointment and failure. Esther Beaney's italic lettering was held up as an example to the class, but she was displeased because it was pinned to the wall beneath a picture of a Virgin with a naked child leaping on her lap, about which she had complained vociferously to her classmates. It was one of the huge Bignall twins who had pointed out primly, as it was inevitable that someone would, that there is nothing rude about the human body, but Esther was unconvinced.

Daisy would sit, disastrous work shielded by her arm, face flushed, heart jangling, longing for a chance to show that she was not of the same poor clay as the other girls bent over their ceramic dinosaurs and bowls of fruit, that she had in fact visited art galleries and exhibitions with her parents, the Royal Academy Summer Show with Daphne in a picture hat, but would not have confessed that her chief memory of Florence was of sitting with her feet in a fountain, eating pistachio ice cream. She had envisaged a terracotta maquette of the Garden of Eden. Alas for ambition allied to clumsy fingers, at the end of the lesson Adam and Eve and the tree were rolled into a ball and she was left with a sad serpent and what might have been an apple. She hung about, hoping that Mr Greengrass would leave the room and she could dispose of her hopeless effort.

'What's this then?' He picked up the snake by the tail. Its tongue fell off. They were alone in the classroom.

'The Garden of Eden,' she said miserably.

'I should have thought that would be more Miss Beaney's thing, but she appears to have turned out a perfectly acceptable graven image of an ashtray.' He flicked his ash into Esther's pot. 'Why are you crying? Do you dislike my class so much?'

'I'm not. I don't.' Through a wet fog of embarrassment she felt a tiny scratch of doubt that he should misunderstand her so, like a piece of grit in the corner of the handkerchief with which she scrubbed her eye.

'It's just that everything I do goes wrong. I mean I have these brilliant ideas and nothing ever turns out like it's supposed to. I suppose I'm just hopeless at Art. I should give it up. I'll never pass "O" Level, will I?'

'Oh, Art,' he said rolling up the snake and placing it on top of the larger ball. 'There, a cottage loaf. How's that?' He pressed it down with his thumb. Daisy laughed.

'I'd better go. I'm missing hockey.'

'But is hockey missing you? What position do you play?'

'Extra.'

'Well, then.'

She traced circles with her finger round the velvety turntable of an old gramophone, part of a still life; silence roared out of its brass convolvulus. Then thudding footsteps sounded, and they turned to the window to see a first-former, red-faced and self-important in her bobbing tunic, pounding up the stepping stones with a message.

'Well, I suppose you'd better cut along to hockey,' he said, with a twisted smile, putting back in his pocket the crumpled pack of cigarettes he had been about to offer. She picked up her bag and left the art room and had to walk in front of Mr Greengrass, her back exposed to his eyes and the wind which ballooned her blouse and whipped her skirt against the backs of her legs.

In the cloakroom she studied her wintry red and purple hands like fuchsias beneath the unerotic grey wool cuffs of her pullover, and her pale unseductive face in the square of glass screwed to the wall.

'What are you doing here?' Esther entered the cloakroom supporting herself on her stick.

'What are you?'

'I've twisted my ankle.'

So they walked together to the sick room, Esther who was in love with Miss Windibank and Daisy who had just fallen in love with Mr Greengrass, the hockey stick between them like a crutch, past the first yellow crocus in a frozen clump of earth.

The feathery grass parted and closed behind Esther as she took a short cut across the fields to visit a sick member of the congregation. She had a basket of goodies in one hand, with the other she tried to pick a buttercup; the strong stem pulled through her fingers, leaving a pink welt across her palm. She was singing softly to herself, without realising it, a hit song which she had heard someone sing at school; the sun was warm on her bare arms, brushed with pollen; she had taken off her cardigan and tied it round her waist. She scrambled down the slope of a bank, steadying herself on the stems of willow-herb, of little buddleia bushes, setting off clouds of butterflies, and crossed the rails of the axed railway line. She laughed as a butterfly settled for a moment on the handle of her basket. Suddenly she stopped. Smoke was coming from the chimney of the deserted station house, hanging in an illicit blue plume against the blue sky.

Esther crept along the weedy gravel between the rails, over poppies and rusty bolts and bits of iron. She set her basket down on the platform and, flattening herself against the wall of the house, edged along until she could see through the window.

On a battered red sofa, half-covered with a bright silk shawl, sprawled Daisy Beaumont, eating an apple and, with his back to her, at the little coal stove, with no clothes on at all, stood Mr Greengrass pouring boiling water from a kettle into a round Britannia metal teapot.

For days Esther was tormented by this scene of shocking

domesticity. The red, green and yellow flowers splashed on the black fringed shawl, Mr Greengrass's naked back view, the round silver teapot. The apple and the teapot seemed in a way the most indecent parts of the tableau, and the sight of a man making the tea, while a girl lay back and watched him. It was inconceivable to her that people could walk around without their clothes on, let alone eat apples and drink tea. She burned with shame. One evening she sat down at the table, pushed back the crocheted runner and addressed a letter to Mrs Greengrass. The following day, after school, she sought out Miss Windibank.

There seemed no alternative to flight. Tom and Daisy spent an anguished night in the station house deciding how to disappear. The morning brought the host of avenging angels.

Of course Daisy could not return to school. There was talk of sending her abroad, but nothing was resolved. Rex and Daphne departed on a trip to the States. Pale, sly and tainted, Daisy spent the summer at St Cloud playing draughts with Finchy.

■ CHAPTER THIRTEEN ■

As Daphne paced the drawing room later that night, while Rex lay in the bed above, she was conscious of pacing the drawing room. She paused in front of a heavily gilded looking-glass to see how she looked when pacing. The verdict was distraught, hollow-eyed, suffering, but beautiful. A black box of cocktail Sobranie cigarettes lay open on the table. She gazed at it. How poignant their colours; soft pink, mauve, yellow, blue and green, lying like pastels in their box. She picked a green one and watched herself, like a dragon, exhaling smoke through her exquisite nose.

Stanley. She poured herself some gin, hoping that the dry spirit would lubricate her eyes and she could weep. She paused in front of the bookcase; the glossy spines of her works in half a dozen different languages brought her no joy. The memory of her quondam fiancé on his knees with brush and dustpan sweeping up the careless debris; at least she had not thrown anything. But did Stanley know that? Had he been watching through the plastic curtain that screened off the kitchen? She poured another glass of gin and pulled back the curtain. The stained glass at the top of the window was quite black. By day it was palest pink and green and yellow but at twilight it absorbed the sky which dyed it deepening hues of blue and green, until it was as the night.

Who was she to be contemplating the nature of stained glass when her brother-in-law was doubtless scrubbing greasy dishes in a crummy restaurant, she asked silently of her mirror-image. She tried to remember their first meeting but could only recall dimly a W.E.A. lecture room and Stanley, who had been taller then, rather faun-like in his tweed jacket and corduroy trousers with his fair hair curling in wispy tendrils round the black legs of his glasses. She had thought until then that a Wykehamist was a member of some Nonconformist sect, like the Plymouth Brethren, or the one to which Esther Beaney belonged. She had been born in a gloomy house all dark oak and mullioned windows and leaded lights, Reigate

Baronial, a ruby lantern glowing dimly and innocently in its porch, where three leather camels marched across the desert of the drawing room mantlepiece and the only literature was the *Radio Times* in its tooled leather cover, which lived in a sort of pannier which smelled of raw camel in the hot weather. Daphne surprised her parents by showing early a taste for reading and writing. As soon as she was old enough she joined the local lending library, immortalised as Smoots by her beloved Elizabeth Bowen. Even *The Death of the Heart* could not have consoled her tonight as she paced the floor, smoke and drink mingling with guilt to disorder her senses. It was when she had read *Dusty Answer* by Rosamond Lehmann she had decided to go to university. Life had failed to mimic art and no one murmured, 'Glorious Glorious Pagan that I adore' of her or offered to put her to bed and bring her scrambled eggs . . .

It was on her last vacation that she had met Stanley. She was working in a factory, making artificial horizons. She thought the lecture might have been about Kafka or Brecht. It was only when Stanley told her, over a cup of tea, that he had nearly completed a novel, that she began to feel a slight interest in him. Then her doormat was snowed daily with letters and poems, half of which she didn't bother to read. He had brought her to this house to meet his parents, 'Boy' Beaumont and the fearsome Ronnie, who, perhaps sensing Daphne's potential all those years ago for turning into a replica of herself, had taken to her immediately. Then Stanley had been sent to prison and Daphne had visited Ronnie and Boy alone. On her second visit Rex had been there. Daphne experienced the sort of shock a person must have when he stands, pen poised over his cheque book in an art gallery and someone else walks in with a canvas under his arm, every brush stroke of which proclaims it to be the genuine masterpiece and the one which he was about to buy a crudely executed fake.

Daphne had sometimes wondered if her defection had been the reason Stanley's novel had never materialised, but always dismissed the thought as a guilty fancy. After all, when he did produce something at last it was that disastrous inferno sequence, and then a feeble collection of decadent poems and eventually, years later a new novel had appeared which she couldn't bring herself to read.

'Stanley will lose his hair,' Ronnie had said, in the garden, snipping the head off a flower. 'But Rex's will always flourish, like a young lion's mane, golden and strong.' Daphne felt like someone in a book as she stood among the raspberry canes beside Ronnie, kneeling in her gauzy dress and wide-brimmed straw hat, a trug of sweet peas like trapped butterflies by her side. The spirit of Vita Sackville West or Gertrude Jekyll hovered very near.

Daphne thought that Stanley's greying wires still clung resolutely to his head, in defiance of his mother. She poured herself a drink, held it up to the light, then reflecting on how little it looked in the big glass filled it to the brim so that she had to suck the surface into her mouth to avoid spilling it. She stood at the window looking out at the black garden. The sound of a distant motor-bike cut into her thoughts; or was it old Finchy snoring?

'Dear old Finchy,' she thought and then was startled by a vision of herself tiptoeing up to Finchy's bed and pressing a pillow over her sleeping face. Shaken, she sat down gulping her gin.

'But I love Finchy!'

'You never loved anyone but yourself,' came Finchy's voice. Daphne started round but there was no one there. She tried a little laugh.

'You're getting morbid, my girl,' she told herself, 'sitting here in the dark, drinking alone.' She drained her glass and sat, slightly dizzy.

'I loved my parents, and Ronnie and Boy and one or two soldiers and Stanley for a little while and Rex and Daisy and Julian – no, delete Julian – and Bryony. So you see you're wrong, old Finchy!'

Finchy's reply was a harsh laugh that bounced off the soft lampshade and cushions and ran up the velvet curtains like a spider. Daphne let her empty glass roll through her fingers to the carpet. She ran to Finchy's bedroom.

'Why do you condemn me?' she hissed, shaking a plump arm that had escaped from the quilt. Finchy moved but did not wake; in the dim light from the hall an ecstatic smile played on her lips, she murmured in her dream.

' . . . taken from this place, to place . . . execution and there will be . . .' Daphne fled.

When at breakfast Mrs Finch brought in the coffee which she needed so badly to slake her parched throat and calm her thumping head, Daphne rationalised to herself that she had merely, her senses inflamed by alcohol, imagined Mrs Finch's voice and had by coincidence stumbled into a dream. Finchy was reassuringly normal in the morning sunshine, her fleshy arm solid as she poured the fragrant coffee, and yet, that sleeve—hadn't Daphne's fingers, when she clutched her sleeping arm, encountered that peach coloured wool?

'Finchy,' she burst out. 'Do you sleep in your clothes?'

Finchy took such offence that coffee erupted from the silver spout, scalding the table.

'I'm sorry . . . I didn't mean . . . I only wondered . . . I often sleep in my clothes—don't we, Rex?' looking at her baffled husband, who had just come in, for support.

'We often sleep in our clothes, don't we? I find it saves so much time in the morning.'

'I've got a splitting headache,' he replied. 'What time did you come to bed last night? I was tossing and turning for hours, afraid to go to sleep in case you woke me up.'

'Your headache can't be worse than mine. Oh don't go, Finchy. Oh, damn! Now she's gone off in a huff!'

'As my head is larger than yours, and my brain weightier, I think we must assume that my headache—'

He broke off as Daphne cried, 'Shut up!' and dashed out of the room.

A house at odds.

'What was she on about, sleeping in our clothes?' Rex grumbled to a fly, as he fished it out of the cream jug and wiped it onto a napkin. Maud's words about Mrs Finch wearing a nightdress over her clothes came back to him. Between mouthfuls of coffee and toast he obtained from Directory Enquiries the telephone number of Carnival Novelties.

'I'm sorry to trouble you, but I'd like to speak to Maud Mandrake.'

'She's in bed,' replied a man's voice.

'How do you know she's in bed?'

'Because—mind your own business!'

'Could you just inform her that she's wanted on the telephone?'

Rex heard the other end of the receiver crash and fall to the floor and then was left like a hooked fish for nearly ten minutes during which he grew more and more impatient, pacing up and down the limits of the flex, tapping his fingers, tearing his hair, whistling and shouting down the telephone and was about to hang up when he heard approaching voices, then the clink of a cup in a saucer.

'I thought I'd wake her with a cup of tea,' came the man's voice, and more faintly, 'Was two sugars right, dearest?'

'It's fine, only could I have a little more milk – hallo – Maud Mandrake speaking . . .'

'Have you found that son of yours yet?'

'Who is this? Oh! Rex, it's you. There's no need to bark like that. Maybe I have and maybe I haven't. What's it to you anyway?'

Rex resisted the temptation, again, to hang up; he gritted his teeth till they hurt and set his head throbbing again. Mrs Finch was dressing the table's burn, which had developed an ugly whitish blister, with some salve or remedy, every ounce of her flesh quivering with displeasure as she rubbed, and Rex tensed the muscles of his calf, clamping his foot to the floor lest it place a kick in the large floral shuddering seat of her overall and send her sprawling among the breakfast debris.

'I'm worried about him. I want to know if he's safe,' he managed to spit out. He closed his eyes and violet-coloured shapes swarmed in the blackness in front of him.

'As a matter of fact he's not back yet, but I did have a telegram saying that he's O.K. The police have been informed but I must say they didn't seem particularly concerned and now, if you don't mind, I'd like to finish my tea before it's cold.'

Rex hung up. He cursed Maud, he cursed himself, he cursed Daphne and Mrs Finch; he cursed that rude, red-headed troublesome boy who should never have been born. However, he crossed his fingers as he cursed this last. The sun streamed through the window, its golden perspective turning his work to dross. His autobiography would be worthless, flat and dull; no one would read it. And rightly so. 'Shut up,' he shouted at a bird. He telephoned Maud again twice. He was informed that she was in the bath; the speaker's own voice sounded sudsy, from a throat full of bubbles. The second time he rang again Maud shrieked:

'Stop persecuting me!' and hung up before he had time to say anything. Outside the weedy garden mocked him, the reedy pool that needed clearing out, the dull goldfish.

'I hope a heron gets you!' he snarled at them, kicking a little stone boy who stood at the pool's edge; a piece of its base crumbled onto the grass. It was a figure Rex loved particularly and he stood, not knowing whether to nurse his own painful foot or tend the injured statue; then he saw that he had gouged a piece of leather from the toe of his costly shoe.

His day was ruined; he would salvage nothing from it. Suddenly for the first time in thirty or so years, he felt a sharp longing for the company of his twin. He set out to walk to Dorking. Daphne flung open an upstairs window and called at his back.

'Where are you going?'

'To do something I should have done years ago.'

'What? What did you say?'

The window sill was stained with golden lichen. Daphne watched a tiny red spider run about on the hot stone and scraped a little heap of dust into a hill and watched the spider's efforts to circumnavigate, and at last, scale it. When she remembered Rex, he had disappeared.

Rex soon had to take off his jacket; a plant caught at his leg and left tiny green balls clinging to his cream trousers. Cowparsley, foaming like champagne, filled the air with a sweet heavy scent; although his prose was heady with the perfume of wild flowers Rex did not know what it was. Only that it pierced his heart with a momentary pang of forgotten childhood, and Daisy's wedding day.

'Some day soon I will be dead and this will all go on without me,' he thought and, spurred on by a terrifying glimpse of an empty green and white eternity, he broke into a heavy run.

■ CHAPTER FOURTEEN ■

'Thud! Thump! Bash! Pow!' Julian looked up dizzily from the comic on the table in front of him into the vortex of his coffee. He was sitting in Acres the Bakers café with Bryony's comic, which he found he had put in his briefcase instead of the newspaper, and its jagged red letters hurt his head. He took the spoon from the muddy whirlpool and sipped gingerly. Something had upset his stomach too. Probably the fish mousse. The thought of facing a Giles Cluff-Trench with dyspepsia added to his reluctance to enter the office.

'Mind if I sit down?'

Julian grunted. There were plenty of empty seats elsewhere. He groaned inwardly at the sight of a large iced bun which the intrusive female was pushing loudly on its plate across the table.

'It is Mr Almond, isn't it?'

He looked up in surprise.

'I thought it was. I hope you don't mind me talking to you. It's all right, I'm not trying to pick you up or anything.'

She laughed. A glance at her, face scrubbed to morning radiance, small eyes relying on their own pale lashes for a frame, hair caught back in an old piece of bandage, made him think that this was probably true.

'How do you know my name? Are you a client? I mean, have I had dealings with you? I'm afraid I don't remember . . .'

'We haven't actually met. I'm a friend of your wife's. An old schoolfriend. It's in the capacity of a friend that there's something I think you ought to know.'

'I didn't know my wife had any friends, at least, she did have one a year or two ago but I had to put a stop to that.'

'The thing is, Mr Almond, or shall I call you Julian, the thing is, I called on your wife a little while ago, not realising that it was your wife, because I've only recently moved back into the district. I've been away for some years.'

105

'In a loony bin, no doubt,' thought Julian.

'I called on behalf of the Saviour, but I found her most unreceptive, as I might have expected, and I promised to call back in a few days with some literature. I did so, rather sooner than I said I would. At two thirty-three precisely in the afternoon I approached the house, namely Fairlawn, and rang the front-door bell. Owing to some noise going on in the house I was not able to make myself heard. I entered the house undetected and proceeded to the bathroom, which I perceived to be the source of the rumpus. There, to my horror, I saw your wife and a soldier cavorting in the bath, spraying each other with the shower.'

She stopped, breathless, and wiped her upper lip with a handkerchief, and took a bite from her iced bun. The woman behind the counter went on buttering bread, slicing eggs, tomatoes and ham for sandwiches.

At last Julian asked, 'How did you know he was a soldier?'

'He was wearing his uniform.'

A ribald snort from one of the sandwich makers made it clear that their conversation had been overheard.

Julian stood up, knocking over his chair.

'Let's get out of here.' They stood outside a fishmonger's shop.

'I'd no idea turbot were so enormous,' remarked Julian. 'One or two of those chaps in the freezer would be a bit of all right.'

Esther, who was more familiar with watery grey slabs of coley backed with sticky black skin, tapped her foot impatiently on the pavement.

He had to drag his gaze from the open counter where the fishmonger was decking the glassy floes with more and more finny and stippled, rosy and rainbowed, shell-tinted, scalloped, sunken-eyed wares, adding the master touch to his display with two gigantic lobsters with coral claws beckoning people to come and buy.

'What did you say your name was?'

'I didn't, but it's Esther Beaney. I expect Daisy's mentioned me?'

'No.'

'Oh! Well, we were at school together. We were great friends. At least we were until she betrayed me.' It seemed to her that she was doomed to be the witness of shameful tableaux involving Daisy.

'You too? You don't know how she betrayed me! Shall we walk on a bit? My stomach's not too strong this morning and the smell of fish isn't helping.'

'Upset tummy? Oh dear! Something you ate I suppose?'

'How did you know?'

'Well, Daisy wasn't exactly renowned for her prowess in domestic science at school! Look, come on, we'll pop into Boots's, it should be open now, and get something to settle your poor old tum!'

Although, despite being brought up as she had been in a patriarchal cult, Esther had very little experience of men, this babying tone of speech and manner came naturally to her when she spoke to Julian. Julian felt tears prick his eyes. It seemed so long since anyone had cared about his tummy.

'What did you mean, Daisy betrayed you, er, Esther?'

He liked the sound of her name, it reminded him of stars on a still night, a tranquil blue and gold vista beyond the horizon of headache.

'Well, ever since I started at the infants school I tried never to have a day's absence, or to get told off, and I kept up my record, right until the fifth year at grammar school when Daisy pushed my face into my custard and I had to stand there in front of the whole school. I was so upset that I had to spend the next day in bed. So bang went my two records in one go. And what was worse,' she panted, keeping up with him as they crossed the road – 'What made things worse was the fact that a mistress whom I very much admired lost her confidence in me and started picking on me all the time after that incident and because of that I failed my mock R.E., which was my best subject, and I got into the most awful trouble at home. Some people might not have got so upset, I 'spose,' she added in a little voice, 'but you see I'd never been naughty so I wasn't used to it. Now sit yourself down in this chair whilst I get something for you.'

Julian sat.

In no time Esther had conjured up a smiling white-coated pharmacist, holding out a glass of white liquid.

'Now, drink this up like a big brave boy, and we'll soon have you feeling as right as rain.'

Julian took the glass, gazing up wide-eyed at her and sipped. It tasted rather pleasant but to please her he made a little-boy face of wrinkle-nosed disgust.

'Do I really have to drink it all?'

'Every drop!' she said sternly and the pharmacist smiled in confirmation. Julian drank wonderingly. What was this conspiracy to look after him?

'I really must get to the office,' he said. 'How much do I owe you?'

'On the house.' Esther smiled at the pharmacist.

'Well, thank you very much. I think I feel a little better already.'

Out in the street which was already busy with early shoppers, Esther said, 'Of course I realised later that it was the Lord's way of chastening me and I cleansed my heart of vengeful thoughts toward Daisy. It was even vouchsafed to me to be instrumental in saving her from herself when, I mean, at a later date . . .' her voice trailed off delicately. 'She made me the butt of all her jokes,' she added, 'and she threw coffee in my face. It's a wonder I wasn't scarred for life.'

This recalled Julian to the reason they were standing together in the sunshine on a Dorking pavement.

'Look!' he said. 'You've got to tell me more about Daisy and that soldier. When can I see you? Are you free for lunch? Good. White Horse at one o'clock.'

'I'm afraid my religion forbids me to enter public houses.'

'Wherever you say, then. I've got to know, however painful it may be, so that I will know what action to take.'

'How about the Gorge? Don't be too hard on Daisy, please. Remember that the flesh is weak.'

Julian looked down into her eyes, pleading for her worthless friend. 'I'll try not to be,' he said gruffly, 'if only because you asked me. The Gorge then, one o'clock. I hope I'll manage to eat something.'

He watched her walk away; not a hint of coquetry in the crisp, knife-pleated skirt that brushed her trim calves, or her small neatly shod feet. He saw that her hair was not bound in an old bandage, but a chiffon scarf whose ends were lifted delightfully by the little breeze. Already, in anticipation, the smell of hamburgers crackled in his nose.

To his surprise, when he entered the office, Giles Cluff-Trench was there, not racked with stomach cramps, not locked in the little lavatory, but spruced and scented and smiling with a pink rosebud in his buttonhole, echoing the healthy glow of his cheek. He clapped Julian on the shoulder.

'Splendid evening, Julian. Please give my thanks to your good lady. She's a charming girl. You're a lucky man.'

Julian sat down, dazed. He realised that he should be entertaining murderous thoughts of his treacherous wife and some soldier, but he sat there with a vacant smile, thinking of a knife-edged pleated skirt and pale hair caught back in chiffon. He called for the telephone directory and dialled his newsagent to cancel the *Beano*.

Julian felt pretty sure that no one he knew would be in the Gorge; he was therefore both taken aback and irritated to see Mrs Jobson and Jenni tucking into large hamburgers, surrounded by piles of chips and beans. He knew at once they had been talking about him from the way a chip fell out of Jenni's surprised mouth when he walked in. He muttered something about meeting a client as he walked past their table; he could see Esther already ensconced at the far end of the café.

'Tummy better now?' she greeted him. 'I managed to bag you a place.' She indicated several carrier bags on the opposite bench. He waited for her to move them.

'You have to order at the counter,' she told him. 'I'll have beef-burger and chips please.'

He had to join a queue and stand for ten minutes in full view of Mrs Jobson and Jenni before he could place his order; the café was getting crowded.

'And a coca-cola,' came Esther's voice through the steam.

It was the first time that she had been taken out to lunch by a man. There was a man in her life, or rather, so much at the side of her life that often she did not think of him from one service to the next when she saw him in his grey raincoat, supporting his mother up the aisle and hoisting her onto the seat of the tiny organ and placing her black-gloved hands on its querulous yellow keys. There was a tacit acknowledgement that Job Harris and Esther would marry when Mrs Harris died; he had told her aunt and uncle, once, in front of Esther, that when this happened he would be free to choose a suitable wife. She had bitten a piece out of her tea-cup. She thought of him now, as she watched Julian's neatly barbered head in the queue, lank hair rising and falling as he plied the wooden handle of the organ as if he was pumping life into his mother's old lungs and if he stopped she would subside in a fusty black heap on the keyboard. Esther mumbled a quick prayer for her preservation.

At last Julian was given a plastic number and was able to return to the table. Esther shifted her bags and he sat down opposite her. Immediately they were hemmed in by two large schoolgirls who took out cigarettes and started to smoke. The beefburgers and chips, a coke and a coffee arrived.

'Would you mind not smoking while we eat?' Julian said to the schoolgirls.

'I don't see a no-smoking sign, do you?' one asked the other.

'It's a free country,' retorted her friend.

'That's what you think,' replied Julian. 'Your headmaster will be hearing from me.'

They exchanged a glance and heaved themselves up, to seek more congenial accommodation.

'That was really admirable of you,' said Esther. 'I really admire a man who stands up for what he thinks right.'

'Well – I – thank you,' said Julian, blushing faintly. The hot food was doing him good; he felt surprisingly better. This girl seemed to cheer him up; then he remembered the purpose of their meeting.

'You said you had something to tell me. Something about a soldier?' Something about a soldier. His mother used to sing that sometimes; for some reason it had made her melancholy, despite being a sprightly little song, foot-tapping even, to the point of inspiring her to do a little dance, which once ended mysteriously in tears.

'You poor man,' said Esther softly through a bite of meat. 'You looked so sad just then, like a little boy lost. I don't know how to tell you,' she went on. 'They say the husband's always the last to know. I don't want to hurt you.'

She rested her hand for a moment on his. Incredibly, tears filled her eyes and she had to grope for a tissue. He hoped fervently that Mrs Jobson and Jenni weren't witnessing this; they'd think he had got the girl into trouble or something. A child in the seat behind him was making disgusting sucking noises with a straw, like bath water running out of a blocked waste-pipe. He half-turned his head. Stanley was leaning across the table, mopping pink liquid from the child's chin. They exchanged a nod. Esther had pulled herself together.

'I'm sorry. I was just thinking of your beautiful home, everything you'd provided for her. There wasn't a blade of grass out of place on your lawn. You deserve better!'

'Better than what? Look, you'd better tell me the whole story.' It took little time to tell. There was a dirty, dull rainbow on Julian's knife. He rubbed at it with a paper napkin while she spoke. She had almost nothing to add to what she had said earlier, no idea of who the soldier might have been, no idea of how long it had been going on.

'I see,' he said, when she had finished, although all that he really did see was, unbelievably, Mrs Finch bearing down on the table with a plate of assorted doughnuts in one hand and a cup of tea in the other.

'I must dash,' he told Esther, standing and catching his foot in the handle of one of her bags under the table. If he stayed a moment longer surely Rex and Daphne and his mother and Daisy and Bryony and the Cluff-Trenches and the cat and tortoise would all appear, carrying heaped plates of doughnuts and beefburgers and chips, and he would never escape. Perhaps he was in Hell.

'Look, give me your phone number, I may need to be in touch.'

'I'm not on the phone. I expect I'll see you . . . Don't say anything to Daisy yet,' she warned and he nodded without knowing quite why and set off up the aisle with a plastic carrier bag dragging behind him, spilling groceries, much to the amusement of Jenni and Mrs Jobson who had reached the gateaux and fags stage; and no doubt of Stanley, for the odious child with him shouted, 'Why has that man got a bag on his foot?' and Julian managed at last to get through the heavy glass door while the whole café behind him rocked with laughter.

Later that afternoon Jenni hovered at his desk.

'Yes, Jenni, what is it? Can't you see I'm busy?'

'Mr Almond,' she began but broke down.

'Mr Almond,' she began again. 'Did you know you had yoghurt on your trousers?'

At this Mrs Jobson could control herself no longer and the two of them had to make a dash to the ladies' cloakroom like two great stupid hippos with convulsions. Julian examined his trousers; there was certainly a little bit of yoghurt on the back of one leg, just above the heel of his shoe; he failed to see how it could occasion such mirth. Strawberry from the taste; was there something funny about strawberry yoghurt that he didn't know? Something rude? Why was he never in on the joke?

A chastened Mrs Jobson, deeply ashamed of her childish behaviour, emerged from the cloakroom in time to see him lick his finger and was sunk again.

'Oh dear!' she gasped to Jenni. 'I don't know what's the matter with me; I've never behaved like this in the office before – never! I mean, it's not really all that funny, when you think about it, is it?'

'No,' agreed Jenni, and they went into fits again.

On the morning after the dinner party Daisy woke to consciousness of shame and foreboding and lay with her eyes shut, trying to locate their source and the reason for the thudding of her heart. Gradually she sensed a space beside her and sat up to confront Julian's empty pyjamas and an incredible smell of bacon and eggs. Then she remembered, her mother-in-law was in the house. She arrived at the kitchen as Julian pushed away a plate of breakfast and pushed past her into the hall. She told herself that the Cluff-Trenches' visit could not make life any worse.

'I hope you don't mind me saying so, dear, but you look really awful,' her mother-in-law said, pouring her a cup of tea and offering her Julian's rejected bacon and eggs. Daisy shook her head dumbly at the plate, sipping her tea. Julian's mother sighed and set to herself, although two smeary plates declared that she and Bryony had breakfasted.

'I do mind,' said Daisy.

'Mind what?'

'I do mind you saying that I look awful.'

She rushed into the garden in her dressing gown, to the empty summer house, to Bryony and the tortoise. By mid-morning a veritable salad had been set before the little reptile. He walked over lettuce, cucumber and tomato and smeared a trail of crushed strawberry through the grass on the underside of his shell. Daisy was recalled to the house by her mother-in-law shouting that she was wanted on the telephone. Giles Cluff-Trench's voice was a blow in the ribs. She had thought it would be Seamus.

'Just calling on behalf of my better half and myself to thank you for a charming evening.'

'How kind,' said Daisy faintly, as the dread hand of memory set the terrible banquet in front of her.

'I particularly enjoyed making your acquaintance again. Funny, isn't it, I never really noticed you before, if you know what I mean.'

'Funny,' agreed Daisy. 'Neither did I.'

'I knew at once we were on the same wavelength,' he said triumphantly.

When she had put down the receiver, Daisy realised that he had asked her to meet him for lunch the following day and that she had accepted. She would not let herself see the full horror of her situation so she sought her mother-in-law's company and engaged her in conversation while she dried the dishes, even as part of her mind, like a television with the sound turned down, babbled silently of dresses and shoes and shampoo.

Later, feeling that she ought to entertain her mother-in-law after she had made the long journey to visit them, she suggested that they might walk down to the pub on the village green and have lunch there, but with such an ill grace that she was refused at once. The prospect of the two of them sitting there on the bench in the sun filled her with dread; she had never been inside the pub and feared that someone might make some remark or joke at their expense. She felt she would not dare enter the bar; besides, did one go into the saloon or public, and once inside she would not know what to order. Added to these worries was the fact that she had no money, except her Family Allowance, and she could hardly drag her mother-in-law to the Post Office first, which in any case would be closed.

So it was with relief that she sat down opposite her at the kitchen table for a light lunch; but her relief was tempered with irritation for she did not eat anything during the day as a rule and saw herself growing gross on the mid-morning biscuits, lunches, mid-afternoon cakes and heavy evening meal that constituted the fuel intake for her mother-in-law's plump little body. She had exceeded her quota during Seamus's stay. How could she, thought Daisy, accept so equably the loss of youth and looks and stand so cheerfully on her little feet, singing at the sink as she washed up? Why was she so damned happy? After all, what did she have? No husband, a son who pretended that she was his wife's old nanny, a dull as ditch water daughter-in-law, whom for all her kindness she could not help but despise, and Bryony. Thank God for Bryony, who could act out her role as grand-daughter with total ease and flair.

Later they walked down to the shop and to meet Bryony from school. Daisy, fitting her pace to her mother-in-law's slower one, watched guiltily as her thin shoes picked their way painfully over the stony path. They reached the bridge over the river and paused, leaning on the rail.

'Isn't it pretty? Just like an oil painting,' panted Mrs Almond, gazing at the elders and flowers and clouds suspended in the brown water, while she dug out a small stone that had penetrated the foot of her stocking. She will expect me to go to Bingo and dances with her, thought Daisy, she will discover that I haven't any friends.

'What's the matter, dear, are you feeling all right? You look as though you've seen a ghost.'

'I'm fine.'

It was the spectre of herself and her mother-in-law tangoing madly in the dusty village hall.

Bryony came sauntering across the green, arm in arm with Jane in a group of three or four other children. Nanny bought ice lollies all round while Daisy slunk miserably outside. There had been no friendly greeting at the check-out, no jolly repartee at the Post Office counter. The children stood chatting and sucking and licking the melting juice which the hot sun sent down their fingers and arms.

'Gis a lick then,' said Nanny and instantly five eager lollies were thrust in her face. Spoiled for choice, her tongue hovered in the circle of coloured cones before making a token dart at each. Daisy turned aside and stared into the litter bin at the heap of sticky wrappers and a wasp balancing on a lolly stick.

'Mummy?' Bryony was waving her green lolly under her nose. She shook her head and had to turn away so that no one saw her face. Nanny noticed the lengths of grubby elastic that trailed from the pockets of several children and on asking their purpose was treated to a display of French skipping in which two children stand with the elastic stretched between their ankles or legs and the others take turns to perform a series of steps and jumps over and under it, each manoeuvre with its own name. Nanny was soon executing a nimble set of variations, skipping in and out of the grey triangles. As Daisy watched the green grass, the chalk hills, the acacia tree, the church spire, rolled behind Nanny's twinkling feet. She attracted quite a little crowd and, face flushed, swept into a low curtsy as she stepped out of the elastic and almost everybody broke into spontaneous hand-clapping.

'You have a go, Mrs Almond!'

'Yes, go on, be a sport!'

'I am not a sport,' she was forced to state but, redeemed by green ice, was able to walk home equably with Nanny and Bryony and Jane who was coming to tea. The worst thing was, or one of the worst things, Seamus would think she had deliberately stolen the manuscript; picked his pocket, betrayed his trust. She could see now that she had done everything wrong. As usual. Her heart felt like a Disprin in a glass of water, that could never quite dissolve; fizzing and fizzing away.

'Come on Julian, sit yourself down, it's your favourite – stew and dumplings.'

'Surely, mother, you must realise that I've moved out of the stew and dumplings bracket?'

Daisy saw pain run across Nanny's face like a drop of water on a hot plate, and then she bent to talk to the cat. The dumplings swelled like clouds, massive. They turned to stone.

'Your mother made it specially for you,' whispered Daisy, although she had known from the way the front door had slammed when Julian came home that she was not to be spoken to that night.

Later, with Bryony's help, Daisy made the tortoise a run where she hoped he might live without Julian's displeasure and a sleeping box into which he at once disappeared, drawing straw disdainfully behind his shelly skirt, and was seen no more that day. Bryony took the fact of his putting himself to bed as a sign of great intelligence and was delighted with him.

'Oh no!' She suddenly clasped her hand to her brow in such a theatrical way that Daisy, alarmed, cried, 'What is it?'

'He still hasn't got a name!'

They knelt in the grass, staring at each other; rejected names fell around them onto the smooth lawn, the few doomed daisies that had dared raise their heads.

'Wait a sec. Stay here. I've got just the thing!' Daisy, fired by her daughter's urgency, ran to the house and took from its hiding place a slim book and ran back.

'*Naming Baby*. Where did you get it?'

'Oh! I don't know, I can't remember,' she lied. 'Look, it gives you lots of names and tells you what they mean.'

As Bryony began to read out the names and their meanings, Daisy recalled buying the book in Smith's in Dorking at a time when she had so longed for another baby that on her walks to the village she had stirred heaps of leaves and old carrier bags with her foot, in the hope that they might yield an abandoned baby, half-believing that her desire would conjure up some unfortunate infant for her to love, as Tom Thumb's mother had found him in a tulip, and that the authorities would allow her to keep it. Julian, of course, could not be allowed to enter this dream. Now the book was kept hidden at the bottom of her sewing basket, with an out-dated Mothercare catalogue.

'What about Arnold?'

'Oh dear, you're not still in the As are you?' Daisy became aware of coldness rising from the earth through the grass and Julian's voice from the back door came harshly, like a black crow, at Bryony: 'Have you done your homework?'

'Quick!' said Daisy. 'Close the book, close your eyes, open the book, put your finger on the page and whatever you're pointing to will be his name!'

His name was Mark.

Bryony had to run in and get a felt pen to inscribe his name on his box. Daisy wondered bleakly if it would be worse, when the time came, as she feared it must, to dispose of a box with his name in optimistic uneven red letters, or the tomb of the unknown tortoise. Her heart was heavy as she carried it to the summer house for the night, especially when she remembered the other refugee who had so recently sheltered there.

She spent as long as she could with Bryony, running her bath, tucking her up, tidying the bathroom; but the time came when she had to go downstairs to brave the floes of silence that would have frozen between Julian and his mother. How she wished, as she steeled herself to open the door, that Nanny had not come to witness their failure; former unhappy evenings seemed almost halcyon before she had come to throw everything into relief. To her surprise Nanny was alone with the ticking of the clock, the cat, the clicking of her knitting needles and a ball of wool that unrolled slowly like time.

'What are you knitting?' Even as she spoke she remembered she had asked the same question earlier and that it was a jacket for a neighbour's daughter's baby.

'It's a little jacket for my neighbour's daughter's baby.' Nanny had evidently forgotten, or was too nice to point out that she had told her already.

Daisy sat down; her bare legs felt cold and under-dressed compared with Nanny's in their sensible stockings. Of course, she would not really prefer to have Nanny's legs, or those brown stockings; they just made her own legs feel wrong. She sighed. Nanny looked up.

'Would you like television on?'

She didn't wait for an answer. The kindly B.B.C., and I.T.V., staging their nightly diversions to save families from themselves . . .

Soon Nanny's head began to nod over her knitting. At last Daisy could no longer keep at bay thoughts of Seamus and the terrible manuscript he had left; they came crowding like dusk at the window. The evidence said that her father must, must be guilty; why did she feel so guilty at believing it? First the fact of Seamus and now this. Nothing was as it had seemed to be. He had made a fool of her. Was anything he had ever told her true? When he had held her when she was little, when he had claimed to love her, was she just an uncomfortable burden on his knees? Knowing his own nature; deceiver, liar, rotten to the core, why had he connived in her own destruction; why had he not rescued her from Julian; helped her to recognise her own nature, rather than watch her live out her days with Julian as gaoler, atoning for ever for her youthful sin? Then, with a sudden jerk she remembered Esther's visit. She uttered a low groan.

'What was that, dear?'

'Nothing.'

How could she confess that she, a grown woman, had thrown coffee in another's face? It came to her that Esther had been an orphan at school and that she had never taken pity on her except occasionally in a facile sentimental way which had not prevented her from being unkind. If only, if only. The clock ticked on. It was almost a relief when a voice broke into her thoughts.

'How many times have I told you not to let the cat on the sofa?'

Julian had materialised.

Blacky, swept roughly off the sofa, woke to find himself in the air, on the carpet. He tried to retrieve his dignity by furiously washing a leg. Daisy thought with a pang that she should have spared him this but had been too wrapped up in herself to move him in time.

Nanny woke with a smile.

'Ah! There you are, dear,' she said, resuming her knitting where she had left off without glancing at the work in her hands. The television reported that two soldiers had been injured in Northern Ireland.

'Good,' said Julian.

His mother looked at him, unable to believe her ears, opened her mouth and closed it.

'I have my reasons for not liking soldiers,' he said. 'My wife, of course, would not agree with me.'

Daisy felt her heart lurch against her ribs. She was clammy, yeasty, wanted to scream.

'Well, I always think that they're some mother's boy,' said Nanny bravely, her voice trembling slightly. 'Come on then, puss, do you want to come up then?' She patted her knee with no regard for her stockings or frock.

'Mother, have you any idea how much those chairs cost? Please don't encourage that animal to ruin them.'

'Well, what do you have him for if you don't like him?' she retorted with spirit.

'I have him, as you put it, because my wife was too stupid to have him destroyed.'

'Oh! Stop it, stop it!' wept Daisy. 'Julian, stop being so horrible to your mother, after she's come all this way to see us.' She ran out of the room to fling herself, like a child, on her side of the marital bed.

'Well, I think I'll be getting along too,' said his mother to Julian, gathering up her knitting and handbag. 'It's been a long day. Good night, dear.'

Julian didn't answer. He flung open the french windows and Blacky ran out into the night, his tail like a bottlebrush.

'Don't bother to come back, you black bastard.' He fetched the vacuum cleaner with much banging and crashing and hoovered the chair and sofa, reflecting bitterly on how he had been forced to give a home to, and spend a fortune in cat food on, that black intruder who repaid him by leaving his fur on the furniture and flaunting himself as if to say: you never get the kisses and caresses that are lavished on me. As if I wanted them, thought Julian, wrenching the plug from the socket and leaving the hoover in the middle of the floor. 'You think I'm jealous of you, you useless black heap of fur.'

A year or so ago, when Julian and Giles Cluff-Trench had been inspecting an empty property they had heard a sound from upstairs.

'Rats,' they had exclaimed, looking at one another, but when they went into one of the bedrooms they found a black kitten, evidently abandoned to starve, too weak to do much more than open its tiny mouth and mew silently, revealing its pink tongue and teeth like specks of ivory. Giles Cluff-Trench picked it up; it lay purring in his hand like a clockwork toy whose wheels have stuck. He was much taken with the little fellow and regretted that he could not keep it himself.

'You can have it,' he said, handing it to Julian.

'Thank you, sir,' said Julian, his virgin upholstery flashing into his mind. 'It's awfully kind, but I couldn't really.'

'Why not? Give it to your little girl. Kiddies love kittens. Pop it into your briefcase and take it home as a surprise. I only wish I could take it myself.'

'Why don't you then,' Julian was tempted to ask, 'instead of lumbering me with it? Give it to your own kiddies.'

He smiled and lowered the unprotesting kitten gingerly into his open briefcase where it made itself at home.

Bryony's reaction was all that Giles Cluff-Trench could have hoped. When she was in bed, Julian told Daisy to take the kitten to the vet in the morning. She agreed and he was surprised to see that she was going to be sensible for once. What, then, was his fury at coming home the following evening and finding the kitten about to rise languorously from a cushioned box and make its way to a bowl marked 'Pussy', which contained what looked suspiciously like cream.

'I thought I told you to take that thing to the vet?'

'Oh! I did,' she answered at once, 'he's had his flu injection and Mr Fraser says he'll be fine once he's got his strength back; he's got to have an invalid diet for a few days, a little minced white fish or chicken.'

'You fool, fool,' he struck her across the face, 'how could I have married anyone as stupid as you? I meant you to have him destroyed, not vaccinated! A little minced chicken!' he groaned. 'How much did that damned injection cost?'

She told him. At that moment Bryony came into the room and hurled herself at him.

'Thank you, Daddy, thank you for rescuing Blacky. If it wasn't for you he would have died!'

Over her head Julian said to Daisy, 'Well, as you've already wasted several pounds of my money on it, I suppose it had better stay. And what was wrong with an old saucer that you had to rush out and squander money on that ridiculous bowl? I'm deducting everything you've spent from next week's housekeeping. And no minced chicken!'

'We haven't any old saucers.'

He had intended to tell Giles Cluff-Trench that the vet had pronounced the kitten diseased and that it had been necessary to put it down to spare it further suffering. Unknown to him, however, when Bryony felt that he had been particularly unkind to the cat, she would stroke him and explain.

'Well, he did rescue you from starving to death, so he must love you really,' and when she felt he had been particularly unkind to her mother or to herself she would remind herself, 'Well, he did rescue Blacky.'

Later that night, their joyless congress completed, Julian and Daisy lay apart in the swampy darkness, listening to the rain. Nasty, brutish and not short enough was Daisy's last thought.

'Daisy?' He nudged her quite gently in the ribs.

'Mmm.'

'Today in the office . . . is there something funny about me? Please tell me, I really want to know.'

She seemed to be asleep. Julian lay awake for a long time. The faint strains of 'Lillibullero' on World Radio came through the darkness from the little transistor in his mother's bedroom, and he felt, as he had nearly always felt, quite alone.

▪ CHAPTER FIFTEEN ▪

Through the plastic curtain, as he stood at the sink, Stanley heard the sounds of feminine laughter. A typing pool's evening out; a hen party. Any moment now, somebody would shout 'Olé.' Stanley slammed a pile of plates into the sink; blotches of oil swam on the surface of the water. He clawed at the surface of a plate and swore as a hard grain of rice pierced him under his nail. The chef was sick with gastric trouble again and Stanley had been obliged to don his white hat and take turns with Carlos at the stove, in addition to washing the dishes and cleaning up, which was his official job. He would be paid nothing extra. An Andalusian dance whirled round on the cassette player and seeped into the restaurant through two speakers hidden in the plastic vines.

'Do you mind if I come in? I won't disturb you. I just want to see where you make all those lovely Spanish recipes.'

Stanley stared dumbly at this intruder who had penetrated the kitchen.

'Do you speak English?'

He shook his head. She was joined by a friend.

'He doesn't speak English.'

'Doesn't look very Spanish to me. Thought they were supposed to be dark and handsome?'

'They are fair in the North, I believe.'

The other, flushed with wine, zip threatening to slide down the front of her bulging trousers, was poking at a pan on the stove.

'Bit primitive.'

'Spain is a primitive country,' her friend pointed out.

'I suppose so, but you'd think they'd try to adapt, wouldn't you? I mean . . .'

'Scusé, where is the toilet? TOILET!' the first was asking Stanley. He pointed with a knife.

'Muchas gratias.'

Stanley sank to a stool, head in hands, and his chef's hat slid to the floor. He tried to think about his novel. The characters were as lifeless as those dull fish gaping on the table. Jason. Mrs Herring. He knew he would never finish it. It was to have been his masterwork, he remembered bitterly. It had shimmered in his mind, full of iridescent images, shining words, a distillation of all his thoughts, everything he wanted to say, mirrors opening one after another, reflecting, illuminating.

The cistern flushed, the door banged. What's the betting they hadn't washed their hands? His masterwork lay drowned in a heap of dirty dishes in the greasy water. When at last he went to clear the tables, Stanley found a handful of pesetas lying on a stained paper napkin on a saucer.

'Are you going to be in that bath all night? Some of us are trying to get to sleep! I have asked you, you know . . .'

'Sorry. I won't be long.'

Stanley tiptoed onto the wet floor; the water spiralled sluggishly down the plughole, protesting loudly. The hot water tank was in a cupboard in Mrs Herring's bedroom and the noise it made filling up kept her awake. Stanley cleaned the bath with a few drops of her shampoo. If it had that effect on the greasy ring of soap, no wonder her hair . . .

In his room, he pulled out his manuscript from under the bed and started to read. It was nothing like the book he had intended it to be. He groaned and took a pencil and started to write. Late at night was the only time he could hope not to be interrupted. He stared out at the roofs, through the uncurtained window, moonlight picking out the stucco and crenellations and unkempt swags of terracotta fruit and flowers. Faintly from the High Street came the sound of lorries. He turned on the World Service on his radio, very low, in case it provoked a banging on the door. Far away in London, Bush House turned up its cornucopia, pouring its riches over the air waves. Two pages were covered with spidery characters. It was awkward holding the cigarette in his left hand as he wrote. He dared not type, of course, lest he tap-tap Mrs Herring out of bed. He became aware of a bumping, a creaking of floorboards and opened his door. Jason on his way to the bathroom in the dark. Gently, so as not to frighten him, Stanley stepped out and followed him to switch on the light. Jason stood blinking, shifting from foot to foot, too much asleep to be able to help himself; besides, his thumb was in his mouth. He was wearing a long-outgrown sleeping suit, stretched to its threadbare limit.

'You'll be bent double if you wear that thing much longer,' said Stanley, as he undid the studs. Jason staggered against him.

'Jason, Jason – what's to become of us?' he asked, as he steadied him.

'Don't know.'

'All aboard the dreamland express, then.' Stanley picked him up, and carried him across his shoulders, and when he laid him back in his bed, Jason was already asleep.

'Jason! Have you wet the bed again?' came Mrs Herring's voice.

Stanley thought of the little figure padding bravely to the bathroom in the dark. He looked at the sleeping child that Providence had delivered into his keeping and stooped and kissed the hot forehead. 'Good night little one. God bless.'

■ CHAPTER SIXTEEN ■

Seamus was not unpractised in the art of letting down car tyres. He and his friends had done it on more than one occasion, in the street or school car park. He was sorely tempted by the Cluff-Trenches' Mercedes as he stood in an impotent rage in the scent of honeysuckle on the drive when he had found the manuscript was gone. It didn't occur to him to suspect that Daisy had taken it; he assumed that it had fallen out of his jacket. He didn't dare to knock again; he had walked all round the house; the windows seemed secure. He straightened up from the front wheel, leaving it intact as he realised that Daisy would be stuck with the Cluff-Trenches all night if he immobilised their car. He picked up a stone, to scrape a vicious gash in the paintwork, then dropped it again; the car looked so beautiful in the moonlight. He was tired; he was hungry.

He had spent an hour or so hanging about the river bank, then had congratulated himself on his luck in hitching a lift to Dorking, whence he intended vaguely somehow to find Stanley. Half-way to Dorking he had realised that he had not got the manuscript or his jacket and was too embarrassed to ask the driver to stop and so was carried on, in increasing despondency, and dropped off at the roundabout on the outskirts of the town with a jovial goodbye from his benefactor, watched the car out of sight, and turned round to walk back. By the time he arrived at Fairlawn, Julian's car was turning into the drive. The stupid sod started cutting the lawn, which anyone could see was so short it was practically bald, then the Cluff-Trenches arrived; no wonder Daisy was dreading them. Then that old lady came in a minicab; he wondered who she was. He had spent the entire evening lurking and at the end of it he didn't even have the manuscript. He could almost wish he was back at school. He was fed up with the lot of them.

'I'm going home,' he said aloud.

Up on the main road the cars flashed past, each dazzle of lights like a blow in the face. He walked along the verge, hoping he was heading for London, with his thumb stuck out until his arm ached. He felt that the whole thing, apart from Daisy, had been a total waste of time. He began to worry about what sort of reception he would get from his mother when he turned up. Either she would beat him round the head or fall on him with kisses. Probably both. How sinister and dark the country was; he hated it; he would be glad to get back to the security of London. His plan had been ill thought out and futile. It was his father's fault for sending him to that bloody school. A thin drizzle which had been dampening his face and shirt swelled into cold gusts of heavy rain. His back ached from bracing itself against the wind; his arm hurt from being stuck out into the road. Water was running down his collar, into his eyes and mouth; his trousers rubbed like wet sandpaper on his legs. He, who had played the urban sophisticate at his new school, was ending his flight as ignominiously as he had started it.

He watched dully as a car slowed down and stopped a few feet ahead of him. He saw twin jets of water spurt from its back wheels; probably a Peugeot. Then he realised that the driver had wound down the window and was beckoning impatiently to him.

'Don't you want a lift then?' he grumbled, as Seamus ran up.

'Yes, yes, I do, thank you very much.' Seamus was almost babbling with gratitude as the driver leaned over to unlock the door and he sank into the warm, cigarette-smelling interior.

'Just a moment,' said his rescuer, looking at the dripping boy, and reached over to the back seat and took two plastic carriers. He had such a round jolly face that Seamus could not be offended as one plastic bag was placed under him and the other behind his shoulders. This process seemed to amuse the driver greatly and provoked a peal of laughter, rather excessive for the humour of the situation, Seamus thought, but found himself laughing too.

'Where to, squire?'

'Well, London really . . .'

'I can take you as far as Tooting. How's that?'

'Great!'

'Cigarette?'

The man flipped two cigarettes from a pack, lit his own at the car lighter and indicated that Seamus should do the same. Then he started the engine and pulled out into the road and they were speeding towards London. Seamus sank back against his plastic bags and drew deeply on his cigarette and studied the driver's profile. He put him at about forty-five; the cheek in view was as red and shiny as a ripe apple, hair like crinkled wheat sprang back from his polished forehead, the fingers on the wheel were as solid as well-washed carrots, soft corn silk fringed his upper lip, and his teeth, when he smiled, were as neat and even as two rows of young corn on the cob; a veritable harvest festival of a man.

'Well! That was a bit of luck.'

'What – sorry?'

Seamus was jerked out of his contemplations.

'I said, that was a bit of luck. Me happening along just then.'

'Oh, yes. Right!'

His benefactor seemed even more pleased about it than Seamus was.

'You like music?'

'Yes.'

'What sort of thing do you go for?' Seamus named a few. 'Never 'eard of 'em! I go for easy-listening type music, myself.' He slotted in a cassette and the car was flooded with the sort of noise that made Seamus shudder if ever he inadvertently struck Radio 2. Then he took out a leather, silver-topped flask, bit it open, drank and passed it across.

'You're right.' Seamus was smiling foolishly as he wiped his mouth and felt the gin swirl like liquid crystal into his empty stomach. 'You're right, it was a bit of luck, you happening along.'

'Help yourself!' He put the flask and cigarettes between them. 'It's a bit late for a boy of your age to be out hitching, isn't it? How old are you, thirteen, fourteen? I bet there's someone at home worried sick about you?'

'No one worries about me. I just come and go as I please. I'm my own boss.'

'Your own boss, eh? I like that! I reckon we're two of a kind then.'

'Yes,' said Seamus, helping himself as bid, 'I used to be in the Army, but I didn't like the life. I'm nineteen, though I look younger. I've seen quite a bit of action . . .'

'I bet you have! I bet you have!' The bunch of carrots was momentarily disengaged from the wheel and gripped Seamus' thigh in a friendly way. Five red marks burned under the wet khaki. A gentle steam rose from Seamus' clothes and mingled with the cigarette smoke and the driver's ready laugh to cloud the windows of the hot metal container in which they swished through the darkness. Seamus fought to keep his eyes open; it seemed rude to fall asleep. He searched for something amusing to say.

'Are we nearly there?' was all that he could manage. The words were distorted by a yawn.

'You have a kip if you like. I'll wake you up when we get there.'

Now that he had been given permission to sleep, Seamus found that he could not. However, obediently he closed his eyes. An image of the black road ahead rose in front of him; cars passed with a little explosion and were gone. Suddenly, he froze, fully awake. Something was stealing over his leg. He jerked it away. The driver's face was more beef than fruit. The air of the fool's paradise turned sickening.

'I – you'd better not come too near me,' Seamus forced the words past his heart which was blocking his throat. 'I mean, I've got an illness. A rash. It might be catching.'

The pink lips churned silently. Then the car screeched off the road and onto the verge.

'O.K. Ginger, it just so happens that I'm a doctor. I think we'd better have a look at that rash, don't you?'

The heavy bunch of carrots knocked Seamus' hand from the door and ripped open his shirt. An enormous knee was pressing him back against the seat. Gusts of gin blew in his face. The easy-listening music poured out.

'Where is it? On the chest or – ouch! you little sod, I'll teach you to play games with me! Seen a bit of action, eh? I'll give you action; nobody enjoys a good game or a good laugh more than I do!'

He gave an eerie parody of his own laugh, and tightening his grip on the torn shirt thumped Seamus back repeatedly against the seat.

'I'm going to be sick!'

'Nobody enjoys a game more than I do, but this is a game where I make the rules.'

The knee ground into him every time he was pulled forward and then he was bashed back against the seat.

'Don't come the innocent with me. I know what you're after. I know what you want, I saw it as soon as you got in the car . . .'

'Sick . . . sick.'

The rage seemed to quiver out of his assailant. He released his hold and slapped Seamus across the face in a disgusted way.

'Bloody be sick then. But not in my car, you don't.'

He opened the door and, thrusting the boy out with one hand, sent him sprawling face downwards in the mud with a kick in the seat of his pants.

'Let that be a lesson to you, you bloody little tease. You've been leading me on all night. Just be grateful that it was me who came along. You might not be so lucky next time!'

The car door was slammed. The car jumped; its wheels churned before roaring away, splattering mud. Somewhere in Surrey, Seamus was sick.

▪ CHAPTER SEVENTEEN ▪

The sky had darkened steadily that morning as Rex walked and, by the time he reached Dorking, it was raining. His feet ached. He sat down on a bench outside the Post Office and watched the women hulking past. Daphne with all her faults had not succumbed to the anorak, that graceless garment, or to the bright orange or blue kagoul, under which the citizens of Dorking hurried about their business like a camp site on the move. Then a pretty girl sauntered past, eating an ice cream, unaware or uncaring that her T-shirt was becoming transparent. Rex sighed and rose.

He had been so sure that he would find Stanley in that he stood gawping on the step when a slovenly looking woman told him that he had gone out. Dimly, he heard her say something about relying on Stanley to look after Jason.

'Are you sure he's not in?' he interrupted her. 'I've walked miles to see him.' She stepped aside to let the bare stairs corroborate her story. A small figure, trailing a dirty blanket, was revealed behind her.

'When will he be back?'

'Search me.'

He thought he wouldn't take her up on that offer.

'I'll wait, if you don't mind. Perhaps you'd show me his room? I'm his brother!' he added testily, as she hesitated.

'I'd have to be blind not to see that,' she retorted. 'Jason, show the gentleman Uncle Stanley's room.'

The child pulled a wet pink thumb from his mouth and gestured vaguely up the stairs with it.

'I was just popping out,' said Mrs Herring. 'You don't mind if Jason stops with you for a few minutes, do you?' And with that she was gone and Rex had no choice but to toil up the stairs after Jason's dragging blanket.

Jason opened the door, which was not locked, indeed had no keyhole, but Rex noticed marks where once a flimsy bolt had been

screwed to the inside of the door and had been removed. Dreariness
fell like slow drizzle from the ceiling and settled on him, on everything. Water from a dripping pipe mingled with the rain and fought
its way noisily through the grating of a blocked drain below. Rex
picked up a small tin of macaroni cheese and read its label.

'I don't like spaghetti,' said Jason.

'It isn't spaghetti, and I was hardly intending to lunch with you.'

Rex looked at Jason properly for the first time. He was, indeed, as
Daphne had said, a beautiful child. His limbs had not lost their baby
look. His shorts had been yanked up carelessly, revealing a twisted
roll of cartoon-printed nylon pants at the waist. The arm that
clutched the blanket was dimpled at the elbow. His belly, swelling
slightly from the frail diaphragm, preventing his short T-shirt from
meeting his shorts, rose and fell gently as he surveyed Rex from eyes
whose deep blue irises were circled with black and centred with gold.
The infrequent use of shampoo had not dimmed the gold of his hair
and the blackcurrant coloured moustache round his mouth could
only emphasise the pinkness of his lips. His twenty pearly nails were
rimmed with black, which gave them the look of banded shells. Rex
felt a brief desire to wash him, to see him in his marmoreal whiteness.
Could he possibly be Stanley's?

'Where are your parents?' Rex asked abruptly.

'Don't know.' Jason evidently did not understand the question. He
replaced his thumb defiantly in his mouth.

'Your Mummy and Daddy. Where are they?'

'Mummy's at work.'

'And your Daddy? Take your thumb out of your mouth!'

'I didn't have no Daddy.'

'Isn't Uncle Stanley your Daddy?'

'No! He's my friend. He buys me sweets sometimes,' he added
hopefully.

'That can't do your teeth any good,' replied Rex sternly.

'He bought me a toothbrush one day, but it fell in the toilet.'

Rex did not answer. He was studying a launderette bag of trans-
lucent blue plastic from which protruded the leg of a pair of checked
cook's trousers.

'Well, go away and play then,' he said abruptly.

'Nanny said you've got to look after me.' Jason evidently had no
intention of leaving Rex alone in Stanley's room. He was jamming
down clumps of Stanley's typewriter keys.

'I can write my name; which is "J" for Jason?'

Rex felt that he had begun to understand the relationship between his brother and this child. He twisted his features into his most menacing glare. 'Go away and play.'

Jason stood his ground, but opened his mouth in a loud tearless howl.

'I haven't got nuffink to play with,' he wailed, taking breath for another roar. Rex took him by the shoulders and sat him down hard on the bed.

'Well, sit there then and be quiet. I may say that your persistent use of the double negative and your malformation of the past participle do not endear you to me. It is not, as you evidently think, cute. So sit there and shut up!'

As he spoke Rex went the short distance to the window and ascertained that the street below was empty, except for a learner-driver reversing round the corner, hopelessly wide of the kerb. He began to poke around Stanley's room, not quite sure what he was looking for. Something – a card, a flower, a letter – which would say that this was not the room of a washer-up and part-time cook at La Golondrina restaurant. Was that speckled glass all that Stanley had in which to survey himself? Well, he supposed it served his visage well enough. He slid his hand down the side of the greasy moquette chair and was stabbed by a broken ballpoint pen, which, when he drew it out, was still quite serviceable. The typewriter, of course, suggested that the room might be used sometimes for a purpose other than sleeping and eating tinned macaroni. Its roller was empty, its keys still stuck up in bunches like the feet of dead insects; but there was a packet of paper behind it. Rex glanced at Jason who lay curled pathetically on the bed with his face to the wall, his blanket draped over his legs, exposing the black soles of his feet. He took a piece of paper and the pen and put them beside him.

'Here you are, you can draw a picture. What did you say?'

'I need my book for leanin' on.'

'Go downstairs and get it then.'

'It's under the bed.'

Rex sighed and stooped down. He pulled a cardboard box from under the bed and took out a book and handed it to Jason who, however, waved it away with a lordly hand.

'What's wrong with it?'

'It's the wrong one. I have to have the one with pictures.'

131

'This one?'

'Just a minute, let me see.' Jason adopted an exasperating professional pose, frowning over the pages.

'Here, just a minute!' Rex snatched back the book and opened it and read:

'To Rex and Stanley, wishing you a very happy Christmas, with love from Aunt Dolly.'

'I thought so! The swine! Half that book's mine!' He turned to the centre pages as if he would tear the book in half.

'W a a a a a a a a a g h!'

'All right, then. You can use it, but remember it's mine! If you get as much as one speck of biro on it, I'll squash you in it like a fly!'

Rex scraped an ancient insect from a page with his nail and returned the book to Jason. The dim bulk of a suitcase in the darkness under the bed loomed in his mind. 'Aunt Dolly,' he mused, as he dragged it out. He barely remembered her. Doubtless she had been fond of him . . .

It was the work of a moment to force open the dusty case. Rex lifted out folder after folder of typescript, pink folders, blue, green, faded almost colourless. He sat back on the floor, surrounded by his brother's mind, his heart beating too fast. There was more stuff here than all the Max Maltravers Mysteries, excluding, of course, the foreign translations.

'I'm writin' you a pome.'

'Make it a sonnet sequence.'

The first folder he dared open appeared to contain poetry. He caught, as he leafed through it, the title: 'To a Child'.

Dawdle through your baby days; toppling towers
Of coloured bricks falling backwards through the years
Dissolve in a rainbow drizzle of tears.

Rein in your rocking horse although Time spurs him on.
Time that breaks buds in April breaks hearts with the same ease
As sets the green haze spinning through the trees

The scent of bluebells drenches the air
A bird calls Stay Stay
Even as he flies away.

'I've finished your pome!'

The begetter of the above was thrusting a piece of paper at him; it grazed his nose. Rex took it. The poem seemed to consist of blue scribbles punctuated with holes where the pen had pierced the paper.

'Most impressive,' he said heavily. 'I admire particularly your choice of metre. No doubt there are marks on the cover of my book which correspond with the holes in your pome?'

'Shall I do you another one?'

'Yes, do. Do lots of pomes.'

Rex gave him a sheaf of paper and, abandoning the poetry, opened what appeared to be a novel and started to read. The bang of the front door closing jolted him. He sat up and closed the folder in one guilty movement and shovelled all the typescripts back into the case and had just kicked it back under the bed when Jason's Nanny's step fell outside the door.

'Come on, Jason, you're missing your programme,' she said as she entered.

'I'm afraid I can't wait any longer,' Rex said. 'Goodbye, Jason.'

'You've forgot your pomes.' Jason slid from the bed, clutching his *oeuvre*.

'Don't be so stupid, Jason. He doesn't want your rubbish.'

'On the contrary, Madam, I am most honoured to have it.'

Rex took the papers and made to take the book but, seeing Jason's mouth quiver, let it lie on the bed. He took ten pence from his pocket and, handing it to Jason, said, 'Buy yourself an ink rubber and get those marks off the cover.'

In the street he looked at his watch. Good Heavens, he had been there for an hour and a half. And never a word of thanks from that woman for minding her grandson. Perhaps there were worse than old Finchy, he thought, as he stuffed Jason's poems into a litter bin. He was very hungry, he realised, as he emerged into the High Street. A bit longer and he would have had to eat that macaroni. The straw-clad bottles outside La Golondrina winked enticingly. He would have to settle for the Gorge or the pub. He was very hungry and very shaken by what he had read. He went into the White Horse.

■ CHAPTER EIGHTEEN ■

As the train lurched into South-West London, Stanley sank lower
into his corner, hunched bitterly against the grey splashed window.
Surely, over the years, someone might have noticed his absence;
might have wondered, 'What's become of old Stanley?' Some
literary editor might have said, 'Stanley Beaumont's just the person
to do a piece on this, or that.' Some hostess might have laid a place
for him at her table, instead of which he cleared the tables of
paunchy parvenus recapturing their trips to Spain. Even Rex – no,
he didn't want crumbs from Rex's table. Max Maltravers! That
transparent, tarted-up imitation of Rex who jetted about the skies in
clouds of cologne, picking up clues a blindfold baboon would have
been hard put to miss, his trusty sidekick never far behind, or in
front, depending on which author's hand prevailed, blowing rings of
feminine intuition from her marcasite cigarette holder, oozing it
from her crocodile handbag and shoes.

It was left to this nobody, the ink still wet on his Eng. Lit. degree,
to dig him up with patronising spade. From time to time an article
appeared in one of the Sunday papers with some such title as
'Where Are They Now?' and Stanley would turn the page with a
thudding heart, but he had never been one of the disinterred. Men
he used to drink with – companions of long afternoons in drinking
clubs: it was as if he had never been. In his agitation he almost
slipped from the seat to the floor. He straightened himself and lit a
cigarette, staring gloomily at the box filled with dead matches – that
would look impressive in the restaurant whose name he could not
remember now. He realised that Martin Timothy was probably not
the smooth egg with dull gold crimped strands combed across his
shiny forehead that he had imagined, but short-haired, in tight
trousers or jeans, like those four laughing youths who now passed
him on their way to the buffet, the very seats of their pants exuding
confidence and scorn. His own trousers flapped as he shifted his
legs; his socks fell round his ankles. Even my socks are losing their

grip, he thought, and made his way to the buffet car, where no doubt he would be buffeted.

He was, and more so when he went through the barrier at Victoria, by suitcases and shoulders and huge hulking rucksacks and a dirty, red-headed boy who seemed to barge into him deliberately, probably trying to pick his pocket. How strange it all is, he thought.

A whole different species has evolved, which carries its house on its back, while I wasn't looking. Light-headed from the two little bottles of whisky he had drunk too quickly on the train, he headed for the tube and then found himself at Leicester Square, standing on the pavement among the crowds like a stone that divides a stream into two currents.

'I'd better have a drink to steady my nerves. Pull myself together,' he muttered.

'You do that,' said a voice, but he could not see who had spoken.

In the French pub, where he had been a familiar face, he was given the cold reception of an outsider. He considered reminding the barman of who he was but sullenly pushed his glass back for a refill. There was still plenty of time before his appointment. What was the name of that man? He found himself wondering what Jason was doing. Ironical, all the times he had longed to be rid of the brat and here he was where he should be, in a Soho pub, missing Jason. The pub was filling up. Stanley was squeezed slowly into a corner, nailed to the wall by a burst of alien laughter. There was nobody he knew; where were all the pretty girls? He was staring morosely at the back of a pair of huge denim thighs whose owner was impaling pale sausages and forking them into her mouth, when a boy superimposed himself between the thighs and Stanley, who started up at the sight of a familiar face, then sank back; he had no idea who it was, but the boy was staring at him as if he knew him. He looked too young to be in a pub anyway. His hair was darkened by rain.

'I've been following you.'

Stanley's bony knees clashed together. The would-be-pickpocket of the ticket barrier.

'Why? Why me?' He tried to sound calm.

'You are Stanley Beaumont, aren't you?'

'Who are you?'

Suddenly the boy's dirty face broke into a smile. 'It's me, Uncle Stanley. Don't you remember me? Seamus!'

'Seamus, my dear!' Something strange was happening to his face; his lips were being pulled back stiffly over his teeth.

'Is it really you?'

'Yeah, it's me.'

'Seamus!'

They stood, Seamus' two hands clasped in Stanley's, who was pumping them up and down. Then Stanley had to drop one hand to dab a finger behind his glasses and Seamus felt a sympathetic wetness stab his own eyes.

'Well, well, sit down, sit down. Let me get you a drink. What will you have?'

'Same as you.'

'Right, right. You sit there. Don't go away, will you?'

He propelled Seamus into an empty space on the bench seat. As he pushed his way a little unsteadily to the bar, Seamus felt a bitter pang of disappointment: 'He's drunk. He's only so pleased to see me because he's drunk.'

When Stanley returned, however, carrying a half-pint of beer and a coke and a cheese roll, such goodwill shone from his face that Seamus felt ashamed.

'It was suggested to me at the bar that this would be a suitable drink for you.'

He handed Seamus the glass shyly.

'I thought you might be hungry.'

The crusty roll on its paper napkin, yellow tongue of cheese protruding, lick of mustard, was the first food Seamus had tasted for many hours. He ran his finger round the plate to catch the crumbs.

'Another?'

'No, it's O.K. thanks.'

'Go on, I'm sure you could do with one . . .'

'Well, if you're sure you don't mind. I – I haven't got any money.'

He blushed and as the embarrassment faded to a pink flush on the white skin Stanley realised what a child he was. He sat sipping his drink slowly while the boy ate. His face was coloured like a white carnation tinged with pink; his eyes, dark-shadowed and slightly puffy as if from lack of sleep, were a true pale green; his fierce hair was as curly as Jason's. Strange how these curly-headed boys should spring up in his path; he realised that he was getting a little drunk and set down his glass with a surreptitious look at the clock.

'Why were you following me?'

'I saw you at the station. I just guessed it was you – from, you know, my father . . .'

'What were you doing at the station?'

'I'd just got off the train.'

Seamus gave a brief account of his journey. How he had seen a plane in the sky coming in to land, blazing like a firework, and then Gatwick's golden globes, nocturnal fruit, rubies and emeralds strung out against the sky, turning it a deeper blue. He did not, of course, use those words; they shimmered in his memory. He half-thought that he might write them down. How he had spent the night in a field and had got onto the station undetected at Gatwick, and waited on the platform at Victoria until he had managed to hide in a group of foreign students and creep through the barrier, wedged between two back-packs, and had spotted Stanley descending from another train. At the place in his story when he described his hitchhiking experience, Stanley interjected:

'You little fool. Don't you know you might have been killed?'

'Yeah, well, he seemed like a nice guy,' mumbled Seamus, suddenly very interested in the sole of his boot.

'But why were you in Dorking in the first place? Had you been to see your father?'

'You could say that.'

'Tell me.'

'Can I have a cigarette?'

'Well, I don't think . . .' Stanley darted a look at the barman, who was occupied.

'Well, all right, although I shouldn't really—'

Seamus started to tell him, beginning at his flight from school and suddenly broke off in his narrative.

'You know those letters you used to write to me sometimes when I was little, well, I used to like getting them.'

'You never replied.'

'No, well, I wasn't very good at writing then,' he said somewhat aggressively, in his own defence.

'Look, Seamus, I hate to have to say this, but I've got a luncheon appointment which is quite important. I ought to go, I'm very late already. Could we meet afterwards? Could you wait? I don't want to lose you again! Would you come with me, and then I'll take you home? Please? If only I could remember that restaurant . . .'

'Hang about, don't go yet. There's something I haven't told you. I've got to tell you.'

Stanley, who had half risen, was pulled back by the boy's eyes.

'What is it?'

'Well, it's about you and my father, sort of . . .'

He had to study the sole of his boot again; it seemed that it was imperative that a piece of grit be probed out.

'Seamus?'

'Yeah, well, the thing is, I know everything!'

'Everything?'

'Yeah, well, I know that he stole your book and pretended that he wrote it!' Seamus picked up the knife that lay on the creased paper napkin on the plate. 'He must be a right bastard to do that to his own brother!'

'I see. And how do you know this?' Stanley spoke levelly; Seamus could see that his hand shook as he lifted his glass and the beer slopped over the lip.

'When I was in his house I found a manuscript in the attic. It was in your writing. It was called "Silence".'

'I see,' said Stanley again. He saw nothing but the past rushing up to swamp him.

'How could you let him? I wouldn't of!'

'It's all so long ago. Put that knife down, Seamus,' he said gently. 'It was very difficult. There wasn't much that I could do at the time. I was in prison, you see; and then he was going to marry my girl.'

'In prison?' The knife clattered to the plate. 'What did you do?'

'Oh, it was nothing dramatic. I was, you wouldn't know what I'm talking about, what was called a conscientious objector. That means I didn't agree with fighting in the war so I was sent to prison for a while and then down the mines. I was probably wrong, I expect I was . . .'

Seamus' khaki sleeve on the table vibrated with implications.

'Where is the manuscript now? Have you got it?'

'I – no, Daisy's got it.'

'Daisy! What does she think of this business?'

'I dunno really, we never got a chance to discuss it.'

'This has all been rather a shock to me. I think I'll have another drink.'

The noise of the pub roared in his ears like a distant sea. He came back with two glasses to find Seamus finishing his beer and lighting another cigarette.

'You'll get us thrown out.' He glanced round timidly out of his spectacles. He had felt himself rise and sink several times in the boy's estimation; now he thought he must despise him. He tasted his whisky and looked at the clock; time in pubs moved at different rates, sometimes the hands of the clock stayed stationary for long stretches and then, turn your back and they would jump forward an hour; as he reflected on this a voice disengaged itself from the general buzz and said clearly, 'I waited an hour and a half in that bloody restaurant – oh, some old Forties figure – ' The rest was lost. The old Forties figure drained his glass.

'What are you going to do then?' He realised that Seamus was waiting for a reply.

'I? Nothing, I suppose. I've done nothing all these years . . .'

He spread his hands in a gesture of defeat. He noticed a brown spot on the back of one of them.

'But you've got do something! He's a thief. He stole your work. He's the one who ought to be in prison.'

'Don't get so excited. Besides I'm not really sure now that it is any good. It was very much a young man's book.'

'No, listen! It's his, your, best book. The others are rubbish. Think of all the money he made. They even made a film, I saw it on telly. All that money should've been yours!'

'All you say is true. In a way. But it could be argued that by keeping silent, I connived in the deception. I'm deeply touched by your indignation on my behalf, but are you sure that you aren't, at least in part, motivated by a desire for revenge on your father for the way he has treated you? I'm sorry, Seamus, really sorry. I shouldn't have said that. I take it back unequivocally. Seamus?'

'Aren't you going to do anything then?' Seamus looked up at last.

Stanley shook his head slowly. 'It's too late.'

'It's not too late. Well, I'm going to do something. I'm going to expose him so that everyone can see what a rotten bastard he is.'

'Don't do that.'

'Why not? Don't you want what's yours by right? Don't you want people to know you wrote that book? I would if it was me. You'd be famous. It would be a literary scandal. Sales of the book would soar. You could be rich. He'd be nothing, like you are now.'

They sat, pushing their glasses about on the wet table. Seamus started drawing in a puddle with a dead match.

'You're very persuasive. It's very tempting, but . . .'

'But what?'
'But I couldn't do it to him.'
'Why not? He did it to you.'
'Because, you see, he's my brother.'

■ CHAPTER NINETEEN ■

A heat haze still shimmered around the green corrugated tin chapel although it was seven o'clock in the evening. Esther thought that beads of sweat gathered in the runnels of its walls like the tiny beads that glittered on her own body. She was late. Inside, the congregation wilted like a few forgotten flowers in an iron greenhouse. Job Harrison, pumping away at the bellows, threw her a glance, tossing a spray of sweat from his darkened hair onto his mother's music. Esther fell to her knees, reddening at her Uncle's fierce stare and her Aunt's little relieved smile. She could feel a bit of grit pressing into her knee as she knelt on the concrete floor. She pressed down hard on it and asked God to chastise her for her impure thoughts. She felt a breaking sensation as her flesh burst through a large hole in her new tights and then a cold circle, with a burning spot of pain at its centre where her knee touched the stone. Try as she might to feel grateful, she could feel only annoyance at the waste of 69p. When she tried to pull the hole higher up her leg, a dozen little ladders sprang up her thigh and ran down her shin. Through her spread fingers she watched her Uncle; small and dry by day as he went about his work in the Post Office, where he kept himself resolutely apart from his fellows, and mimeographing the smudgy leaflets which Esther distributed and which had of recent years brought in not one soul to swell the diminishing congregation, he burned only in the greenish light that the trees threw at the wire-meshed chapel window. The ladies of the church were forbidden to take paid employment outside the home so Esther existed on a small allowance from her Uncle, with which she was expected to clothe herself and pay whatever fares were necessary for her missionary work; when she could, she walked.

At this moment, her Aunt was thinking that she must get a wire brush and scour that wire mesh through which the light fell so prettily dappling the floor. She accepted unquestioningly the hard faith into which she had been born. If ever she sighed for pretty clothes, the cinema, a television, a radio even, no one had ever heard her. Her fingers were as hard and yellow as the soap with which she scrubbed the floors of the little house which they had shared with Amos's parents and continued to occupy after their death. Carpets were a vanity, curtains were heavy necessities, sewn by Amos's mother, to be taken down twice yearly and washed in the bath. This had been one of Esther's treats as a child; she had run up and down the bath, the humped curtains squeaking under her bare feet like friendly whales. Esther had come to them when she was two, orphaned when her parents perished while doing missionary work. The Church of the True Faith was not without its martyrs. They had eaten contaminated corned beef in a temperance hotel and died within hours of each other in a Liverpool hospital. Hannah, who had no children of her own, accepted her husband's brother's child and counted her as her greatest blessing. Had she been born a Hindu, when the time came, she would have gained much pleasure from selecting the material for, and sewing the sari which would melt round her as, after rubbing her hands together and commenting on the lovely blaze, she leaped cheerfully onto her husband's funeral pyre.

'O God unto whom all hearts be open, all desires known and from whom no secrets are hid . . .'

Fragments of her meetings with Julian shifted through her mind; she saw his neat hands with their polished nails on his knife and fork, his full lips puckering on the glass of medicine in Boots, smelled again his faint tang of citron. She had almost cried when he had caught his foot in her carrier bag and everybody had laughed at him. She pictured the dry figure of Miss Windibank, like a conifer spreading its sparse branches over her girlhood. Daisy had turned Miss Windibank against her, and she had Julian, whom, of course, she did not value. Daisy had always had everything, and valued nothing. Just contrast her and Esther's homes. Greedy and careless and valuing nothing. . . .

Esther felt Uncle Amos's eyes upon her.He had sniffed out her sin as a wolf scents blood; head lifted back, he almost bayed at the bare fly-spotted bulb swaying very slightly on its flex in a faint draught that must have come from the window or might have been an involuntary sigh from the harmonium. How could he know, when she hardly knew herself, that she had fallen in love with a man who was not of their Church and therefore unclean and doomed? But know he did, as did her Aunt who knelt beside her on her grey print frock, her hair captive in a net and pierced with pins. They had sensed a moving away from them. At supper yesterday Esther had watched the muscles jumping in her Uncle's temples as he chewed his cabbage, had tried not to dwell upon the grey mutton, reinforcing her Aunt's gristly tissues. Cabbage boiled colourless; hair trapped and pinned lest it grow rampant and rampage. The knots of the cotton scarf that covered her own hair tightened at her neck. She had begun to suspect that flesh need not be grey; that it might be luxuriant. Voluptuous naked ladies, like pink and white clouds tipped with gold, drifted across the ceiling. Esther shivered; the green light muted her burning face. She pulled her cardigan close to her and felt her ribs, fragile yet enduring; it was the flesh that would fall away. Her heart hurled itself against the bars like a bird that had just realised that it was caged.

'I must get some fresh air – the heat,' she whispered to her Aunt's hair, as she rose and hurried into the night, leaving a draught of shock in the chapel behind her. The day's heat, stored in the pavement, rose through her shoes but a wind billowed her skirt and the trees. The leaves, glazed and uneasy, showed their undersides like animals laying back their ears. Esther groped in her handbag for a tissue and pulled out a clutch of leaflets; the wind took them from her damp hand and carried them away.

Esther could give no satisfactory explanation for her behaviour.

'Oh, shut up and leave me alone,' she screamed at Uncle Amos in the kitchen and rushed up to her room.

'I ought to beat some sense into that girl.'

Aunt Hannah placed her hand on his and dissuaded him. She did not think Esther deserved a beating, and besides, being a practical woman, she knew that if he took off his belt, his trousers would fall down.

Later that night Esther was woken by strange rumblings behind the thin wall that separated her bedroom from that of her Aunt and Uncle, and groans like grey smoke in the blackness. Through the wall she saw her Uncle on his hands and knees chewing the carpet, wrenching out tufts with his teeth, like Nebuchadnezzar eating grass, worms writhing in his beard. She switched on the light to dissolve this disturbing phantom and her door opened. Her Uncle stood, darkness behind him. His thick white pyjama jacket, buttoned to the neck, was soaked; his bare feet gripped the carpet. His face was bleared with tears and one, hanging in his beard, caught the light and sparkled.

'Esther, I've had a vision.'

She realised that the tears were not tears of grief. Her Aunt appeared behind him.

'A vision?'

Esther shivered and buttoned the top button of her nightie as she felt cold sweat start out on her body.

'I have seen the end of the world. I have seen the ungodly perish in flames, Esther.'

He gripped his wife's arm. She did not cry out but Esther saw the fingermarks on her arm reflected in her face.

'That day, in whose bright, clear, shining light all wrong shall stand revealed . . . The Day is at hand!'

He fell to his knees. His wife fell to her knees in the little passage behind him. Esther sat staring at them. They might have been a pair of old familiar chipped salt and pepper shakers for all she felt as they knelt there in their white garments. Then she realised they were waiting for her, so she swung her legs over and dropped down beside her bed, burying her face in the rough thin blanket. The light was red, streaked with yellow, like hellish fire, then she pressed her fingers to her eyeballs and the blackness quenched the flames and the little specks and stars of coloured light swarmed across the black, gold and silver cells split and fused; they were light, they were life . . .

' . . .deal not too harshly with her, Lord, scourge her with many rods, as Thou must, but admit her at last to Thy Grace—'

'No,' shouted Esther. 'No. It's not fair! It's not fair! I don't want to die!'

She bit her pillow; the old cotton pillowslip tore in her teeth; she felt the ticking cover tear, feathers plunged into her wet mouth. Her Uncle took a step towards her, his arm raised; his wife grabbed his arm so that the blow fell lightly on Esther's shoulder. Heedless, she bit and tore, sobbing and crying.

'No! No!'

'I'll make some hot milk,' said her Aunt.

'The time for hot milk is past,' said her husband, but he followed her to the kitchen.

When they returned, with three thick white cups of thick white milk on a tin tray, painted with pansies, now more gold than black and purple where the paint had worn off, Esther turned to face them, her face blotched and swollen, feathers stuck round her mouth in a parody of a beard.

'When?'

'Drink some hot milk, dear, you'll feel better,' replied her Aunt. Esther took, obediently, the proffered cup.

'When?' she asked again.

'Next Wednesday, dear, so that gives us a day or two.'

'Next Wednesday!'

'Do wipe those feathers off your mouth, dear, you'll choke if one gets into your milk. I suppose I'd better cancel that appointment at the chiropodist's,' she added. 'Oh dear! There's such a lot to do . . .'

'There is nothing to do but pray.' The patriarch spoke out of his own beard.

'What's going to happen?' Esther dared to raise her eyes to his, then dropped them to watch her doom framed by those glittering lips.

'The chosen must assemble at a high place, where they will spend the night in prayer and repentance and in the Dawn shall come the armies of the Lord and all shall perish and only the righteous shall be granted eternal life, so repent your . . .'

'Leith Hill,' said his wife.

'What?' he asked testily.

'Leith Hill. We could go to Leith Hill. That's a high place. You like Leith Hill,' she said encouragingly to Esther, who had started to cry again. 'Remember when we had that picnic there? Only I don't suppose the tower would be open at that time of night.'

'What tower?' roared her husband.

'The tower on Leith Hill, of course.'

It seemed that a feather had got into Esther's milk as her Aunt had feared, for she was gasping and choking, her milk rose up in a white geyser, engulfing her mouth.

'Pull yourself together, woman,' said Amos, looking at her with disgust. He switched off the light and his wife followed him to their bedroom, but outside their door she turned and called, 'Try to sleep now dear, or you won't get up in the morning.'

As they switched off their own light they heard a low cry or groan: 'Julian.'

'Julian? Who's Julian?' Amos accused his wife. 'Do you know of any Julian?'

Then, the darkness was made uncomfortable by her sobs and on a single impulse they pulled the blanket over their heads.

Esther's tears gradually died away. 'I don't believe it,' she said defiantly. Then it dawned on her that truly she did not believe it. She lay on her back, her heart thudding at its own daring. If it should be true, what a time to lose one's faith. But, she realised, it was not God in whom she had lost her faith, but Uncle Amos. She saw him suddenly as a sad, silly, disappointed old man who had engineered a dream to justify his own life.

The fear of everlasting torment was very real to Esther but she writhed in the bed in a torment of itching; her elbows turned to red circles of irritation, then her upper arms itched, her legs, between her shoulder blades, she felt as if she was rolling on crumbs, with little red worms burrowing under her skin. She scratched and wriggled, her burning flesh blotting out her guilty picture of her Uncle, making it impossible for her to think of anything but cooling it. She was soon covered in weals like white worms for she had skin that marked easily, and had made much moral capital of it at school. At last she subsided and forced herself to lie still with her winceyette nightdress in a clumsy tangle round her waist and the elastic of her night knickers biting her leg. They were, in fact, old school knickers, faded to the colour of boiled cabbage, which seemed to have found the elixir of eternal youth. A runnel of sweat trickled down her breastbone. For a second she had a desire to tear off her clothes and stand at the open window letting the night air wash over her skin. A woman in a paperback book Esther had once found on a bus had done this, and had also stood naked gazing at her reflection in a cheval glass. There was no looking glass in Esther's room. She had crammed the book into the used tickets receptacle as she left the bus and descended the steps on trembly legs and stood on the pavement in a daze, blinking at the temerity of a woman who would do such things, the shamelessness of a person who wrote of them. She blushed for the printers, the publisher and stared at the mad bravery of the people strolling out of the shop in front of which she stood with cigarettes and pieces of the gutter press in their hands, as if W. H. Smith sparkling in the sun was not the gateway to the fires of Hell.

Perhaps Julian was the Devil, come to put her to a final test. She pictured horns sprouting from his pale forehead, gleaming with a faint grease of anxiety, a forked tail swishing from his neat trousers. Stupid. She began to itch again, grinding her face against the abrasive pillow. 'Please God don't let the world – ' she choked at the thought of her tiny voice pitched against principalities and powers. Her narrow room was like a cabin in a ship she was powerless to stop, speeding across a black sea. She thought back on her joyless life; birthdays without presents or parties, she had had to keep them a secret at school lest anyone should ask what she had got; bleak Christmases without decorations. Once, as a small child, she had hung a branch with milk bottle tops. Her Uncle had been quite kind as he had snapped it in half and thrust it, jangling, into the dustbin. It had not been very pretty, anyway. She had had no cat or dog or even a doll of her own to love. She had fed the birds in the garden for a time but they flew away squawking from her over-eager peltings with crumbs and would not be tamed. Although not exactly unpopular at school, she had always stood apart from her fellows, an oddity in her too-long tunic, on the edge of their games and jokes, hung about with the faint odour of her alien life.

Now she was in danger of losing her soul without tasting any earthly delights. It was not God she doubted, but her Uncle's vision of the Apocalypse. Why on earth, from all the religious leaders of all the Churches in the world, should God choose him? Surely the Church of the True Faith couldn't really be the True One, although for nearly thirty years she had believed it to be so. She had read no philosophy, no theology; all she had to go on was the rigid dogma thumped out in corrugated iron. She had to remind herself that certain events took place in a stable. She realised that her doubts were not really all due to her meeting Julian; she had been going about her missionary work with increasingly less conviction. She was simply very tired of having doors shut in her face and very weary of walking about the world alone. Esther pushed back the sheet and fell to her knees on the linoleum; she was assailed by the sharp, cheap scent of the talc she had sprinkled into her wide black shoes to freshen them for tomorrow's trek.

CHAPTER TWENTY

'How terrible the morning light is, when first we wake and must grunt like pigs in the debris we have made of our lives.'

Water poured from the tap and splintered gold and silver in the sink and on the draining board. The gas rings's blue coronet of flame was almost quenched by the sun. Daisy stood in the kitchen in her dressing gown; the hard white surfaces of fridge and cooker hurt her eyes; she had been elsewhere in a dream for a few hours and had been brought back to face all her failures in the morning's clarity. Julian had left. Nanny was still asleep. The bread-knife showed its teeth in a silver snarl; she picked it up and tested its bite along the skin of her arm but was stopped by Bryony's voice.

'Professor Blacky has come to see you.' She was carrying the cat, who was wearing her grandmother's glasses, over her shoulder so that their faces were on a level. The round black face with glassy eyes stared through the lenses until they slipped.

'What's he a professor of?' asked Daisy.

'I don't know. What do you think?'

'I think he's writing a learned paper on the effect of the cat's claw on the towelling dressing gown.'

Bryony looked. The shoulder of her dressing gown was a mass of pulled threads.

Daisy had thought that the roar of the hoover could absorb her howls of despair but she found that her eyes and throat remained as dry as the hall carpet that she was attempting to rid of the microscopic specks of thread and grass that Julian's trained eye would home in on when he returned. He was at work, Bryony at school; how she envied them having somewhere that they must go each day; Julian's mother, saddled with the dullest daughter-in-law on the face of the earth, had taken herself off to Dorking on the bus. Daisy knew she should have gone with her, taken her out to lunch, but Julian had given her no money, as part of the punishment for the Cluff-Trench fiasco, and she did not even have the bus fare. Seamus was God knows where. Blacky was glaring at her from the top stair, expressing his disapproval of the cheap cat food which mouldered in a pink heap in his plate, attracting flies, and obviously he expected her to conjure prime fish out of the freezer, the fridge or the air.

'Can't you understand plain English after all these years?' she had screamed at him. 'There isn't any. No fish! If you're really hungry you'll eat what's in your plate!'

He wouldn't, and if he did, she knew, he'd be sick. The tortoise was sulking in the garden. The sun lurked somewhere behind tightpacked clouds.

She rammed the hoover into the corner to get a recalcitrant piece of fluff, an instinct made her pull it back, too late. A wounded green lace-wing insect rolled there in whatever agony such broken filigree legs and wings could feel. She switched off and picked it up and carried it, weightless and heavy as lead, to the garden and left it there.

'That's what comes of hoovering,' she told herself.

The memory of her crime rose to the surface of her mind. Nowadays it was increasingly difficult to push it under again. She drifted into the bathroom. A fly sat on the rim of the bowl rubbing its hands. She caught sight of a distraught face hanging in the mirror of the bathroom cabinet.

'What are you staring at, you hideous, useless lump?' said the face.

She drifted out again; into the bedroom where her mother-in-law slept. She dared not enter lest her heart be pierced by some too poignant possession. Blacky hunted her through the house. She thought that she might prepare some vegetables for the evening meal. She raised the knife to a carrot, but how to flay one in the presence of its fellows? Like taking a prisoner and leading him to the dread courtyard and killing him slowly in front of his fellows who knew that in a moment his screams would be theirs. She threw the carrot down. Nevertheless the tortoise must eat; and so, she supposed, must the rest of them, even she must fuel her carcass to drag itself through its pointless days to the inevitable judgment. Esther Beaney had come, stirring up her mind with thoughts of death and Hell. She wished she could die now and get it over with. She had thought often of confessing to a priest, but absolution would not bring back the woman she had killed.

She had never understood how a convicted murderer could, on

release from his sentence, say, 'I have paid my debt to society.' Her worst fear was that Bryony would find out someday what she had done. That would be her eternal torment.

She plunged a cabbage into cold water and started to remove its outer leaves to tempt the tortoise. She stared into the basin, or sink, in the manner of the poem, and a tiny grey drowned slug floated from under a leaf. That's what comes of cooking.

In the garden she took off her shoes to feel the short grass under her feet. She inspected the washing on the rotary drier, an ugly blue spider web which Julian had planted in an obscure corner so that a washing line would not offend the eye. The outer garments were dry, those nearest the central pole were heavy and dank. She gave it a push, spinning their accoutrements round in the windless air. If only she had something to do, something to stop her mind running round and round on self self self like the rotary drier.

A white fluttering; a butterfly trapped in the greenhouse, battering at the glass, thinking it air, unable to understand why its element should deceive. She managed to catch it and looked at it as it lay quivering in her hand; black veins striated its white wings; its head was blurry and soft. She released it and watched it fly away and stepped back into the hot moist air. The glass walls shimmered with tiny droplets. A bead of water rolled from a leaf at her fingers' touch and broke like mercury on the earth. She leaned back on a shelf neatly stocked with a deadly arsenal of aerosprays and balls of green twine and the secateurs in their polystyrene box, breathing the sweet-sour scent of tomato leaves, the fruit hanging in heavy green and red-gold clusters. A butterfly, another cabbage white, lay on an open gro-bag; the wings were still perfect; whatever life was, the current that had charged through the veins was, it had gone. Suddenly the glass could not protect; shame was filtering through the panes, the little hairs on her arms stood up like the hairs on the tomato stalks. Seamus. He was just a child. She had exposed all her weakness and cowardice to him. She had let him go off into the night. Fate had sent him to her and she had treated him no better than a baby hedgehog which had died in its box in that same summer house.

'The murderer chalks up another crime,' said a voice. Ah, yes, the murderer. She had to face it now. There was no evasion of conscience's bright spotlight in her face in this hot cell.

'Do you recognise these exhibits; these empty bottles, these tablets, stomach pump?'

'Yes. Yes. Yes.'

She sank to the ground, the warm damp earth oozing through her fingers; a worm rose from the grave and slid across her face.

Slowly, slowly she became numb and then slowly little green tendrils curled from her fingers and toes and branched out from her body and head, unfurling themselves to the kind sun.

■ CHAPTER TWENTY-ONE ■

'Excuse me, I happened to notice that you put a tube of Smarties into your shopping bag.'

Julian's mother turned to face her accuser in Sainsbury's, blood draining from her face. A fellow shopper baulked, nylon flowers flooded her senses, blocking the shelves; she swayed.

'Are you all right?' The tone changed to reluctant concern.

'Are you feeling all right?' The words came from far away through the pounding of her heart.

'Yes, yes, thank you, I'm fine. Just a little dizzy,' she heard her own voice reply. 'A momentary dizziness. Smarties, did you say? Oh, here they are – for my granddaughter.'

She fumbled the tube from her bag and put it in her wire basket. 'I don't know what came over me. I've got a lot on my mind. You won't tell, will you?' Her voice shrank to that of a pleading schoolgirl's and struck some chord in the other's heart.

'Well, O.K., I won't,' she said gruffly. 'But I really think you should go home and lie down. You don't look at all well.'

'I will. Thank you.'

Once safely through the checkout and out of the door she panted a few paces down the road and then leaned against the window of a dry cleaner's. A giant teddy-bear in sunglasses stared out at her.

'Stupid woman. As if I would steal a tube of Smarties!' she permitted herself to censure. Nonetheless it had been a narrow escape. The truth was she had felt jumpy all morning; ill at ease, a sense of something wrong; as if she must hurry back. That was why she had stuffed Bryony's Smarties into her bag. If she had been caught . . . Julian's shame. Bryony and Daisy, she felt, would forgive.

'My wife's old Nanny . . .' she said aloud as she hurried to the bus stop. She found, when she consulted the timetable, that she had forty minutes to wait. Forty minutes! Panic stretched them out like grey chewing gum. How could she get through forty minutes? How else but with her small neat feet planted firmly on the pavement, with the traffic pouring through her head. She could not help but notice that all the passengers on the bus were pensioners, all but one young girl with a push chair, which she gave her a hand up the steps with. The driver had to get out of his cab to hoist aboard one old boy with two sticks, one painted white, and a heavy shopping bag.

'It's a shame. They shouldn't let him out,' she heard and the words struck a chill to her heart. Julian would put her in a Home. 'I'll go over Beachy Head first!' That first night, in the spare room, she had packed her bag ready to leave in the morning. If it hadn't been for little Bryony, and Daisy. She could see things weren't right between her and Julian but she was so cold, so aloof, it would take an ice pick to hack into her heart.

The bus was passing over a stone bridge, 'Deepdene Bridge' it said on the side, and red and white cows were wading into the river to drink. 'Oh, hurry up, hurry up,' she begged silently as they lumbered on behind a tractor. Her fellow passengers' noise was intolerable, the jabbering and cackling that came from those old heads, that once belonged to boys and girls in the playground. They would all be dead in ten years! Once the G.I.s had called her 'Blondie' and what now, what now? Raindrops rolled down her thick white mac, generations of children skipped over the crossing under her guiding lollipop. The countryside oppressed her; she could not understand how people could spend their whole lives travelling between fields. All she could do was wait, and be there if ever Daisy decided to come to her. She thought that she would knit her a jumper, the poor girl seemed to have so few clothes.

Mercifully her bus stop hove in sight. She pressed the bell with relief and then stepped down, thanking the driver, as she had observed was the custom in these parts, onto the verge, a little townswoman, bracing herself against the barrage of grass and sky and the stones on the path that would pierce her feet. Beachy Head loomed in her mind; it must be the influence of this melancholy place that inspired thoughts of the road across the cliffs where the wind had combed the bushes into stiff green pompadours against the sky like a pearly shell. She would not let herself dwell, but instead con-centrated on Fairlawn's green aspect. The curtains that swished along the tracks and seemed to shut in, rather than out, the night. She braced her shoulders and reminded herself that she had years of active life in front of her.

'Ooh, ooh,' she called cheerily at the front door, 'I'm home!'

Silence bulged against the little panes from within. Bees buzzed in the honeysuckle bower. She gave the door a push and it swung open, releasing a pent wave of emptiness that engulfed her.

'Something's wrong; something's wrong, I knew it . . .' she muttered, as she ran from room to room, leaving doors swinging in her wake, then out into the garden onto the tilting lawn, past the tortoise, past the cat – 'Where's mistress, boy?' – to the sunny cedarwood summer house standing open and at last to the greenhouse, where a shape through the glass stopped her in her tracks. 'You're a silly old woman,' she said aloud, panting on the grass and had to stand to catch her breath before strolling down to the greenhouse. When she stepped into the greater heat, the greeting died on her lips, 'Whatever are you – Daisy, wake up! Daisy! Say something!' She pulled at her arm and shook it. It lay as heavy in her fingers as wood.

Her fingers fumbled at the pages of the telephone directory, then the names buzzed on the page like so many insects; she had to go and get her glasses, then she couldn't find their name, of course, they would be ex-directory, the snobs. She dropped the book onto the floor and gazed round, distractedly. Her eye lit on an address book by the telephone and she found the number. Daphne answered. 'You'd better come at once,' she heard.

Daphne's long legs overtook easily as the two women ran down the garden. Daisy had risen and grew, streaked with earth, half-naked, feet firmly in a gro-bag against the glass.

'I'm going to ring the doctor. Button her shirt.' Daphne ran back to the house.

Daisy was borne away in an ambulance to be transplanted into the healing soil of a hospital.

The two mothers sat in the hospital corridor.

'Julian's not at all like you. Does he take after his father?'

Nanny dropped her voice a tone.

'Well, Grandma, I never knew his Dad that well. Not intimately like.'

Daphne nodded understandingly. 'I think, don't you, that we should stop calling each other "Nanny" and "Grandma"? I'm Daphne.'

'Grace,' said Nanny. Daphne took out her cigarettes and offered them.

'We'll get told off,' giggled Grace, but she took one. A foreign orderly in a green overall was drawn out of a door by the smell. She pointed angrily to the 'No Smoking' notice above their heads. Daphne answered with a voluble flood of Spanish and the foreign person, whether she understood or not, blanched and retreated.

The notebook in Daphne's handbag would remain closed, the silver pencil sheathed; Nanny would not be used as raw material, for Daphne, to her astonishment, found that she liked her. A nurse came out carrying an empty glass on a tray.

'I got her to drink something. I told her it was phosphate. She thinks she's a plant,' she added defensively.

▪ CHAPTER TWENTY-TWO ▪

It was dark by the time Seamus arrived at 'The Magic Carnival Novelties'. Had he known that the money Stanley had given him for a taxi meant that his Uncle would spend the next day *sans* Camp coffee, *sans* cigarettes, he might not have spent it on a cinema ticket, but he hadn't known and now that he was so nearly home he was afraid to face his mother. The flat about the shop was in darkness, in contrast to its neighbours. When he fitted his key in the lock and then groped his way upstairs to the sound of Geoffrey fumbling with a fusebox, his mother was in bed, glimmering faintly in the light from the window.

'Oh, it's lovely to be looked after, but he's a bit predictable—'

'You mean he keeps putting spiders in your tea?'

'Right!' She laughed delightedly and patted the sheet. 'Here, snuggle up to me like you used to and tell me what you've been up to. What do you think, he wants to make an honest woman of me, Seamus, but I don't know – I don't know if I'm ready to settle down – the old life calls me. He thinks that together we might make the business a going concern. I don't know if domesticity is good for my art – I haven't written a poem for days. I was thinking, I might change my name to Maeve, or Mebh, except that I can't spell it, what do you think? Got any fags on you? Oh, Seamus, I'm glad you're back! It's so dull here!'

A sound like a pistol shot fragmented her last words, then another and another – a volley of shots.

'My God! He's shot himself!'

Maud and Seamus ran or fell downstairs in the darkness; a blazing rocket swooped past them from the shop. Seamus pulled Maud back and then had to flatten himself as red zigzags, hissing and exploding, ran across the floor to attack him in a smell of gunpowder and burning paper; from the heart of the fire burst silver stars, golden rain poured to the floor, cascades of stars and sparks, crackles, bangs, bursts of blue and green and in the middle of it all, the huge black figure of Geoffrey, beating coloured fire from the air, stamping jumping jacks under his feet. He had dropped a match into a box of last year's fireworks.

'A bit previous aren't you, mate?' said a fireman cheerfully. 'It's only July, you know.'

'I'll make some cocoa,' said Geoffrey shakily.

'Cocoa.' Maud made a face at Seamus behind his back as Geoffrey, his clothes full of little holes, his face streaked, his hair in sooty spikes, lumbered towards the kitchen. Although his fingers dangled like bunches of burned-out sparklers, he was not hurt, just black and shocked.

'I'll make the cocoa,' said Seamus. Geoffrey, blackened excelsior tangling round his feet, in the light which a kind fireman had restored to the shop, gazed desperately at Maud. 'I don't suppose you'll want to stay with me now. A great clumsy oaf like me . . .'

'Oh, I don't know. At least it won't be dull.' Maud gave the lie to her answer with a yawn.

After the firemen had left, Seamus staggered upstairs, so tired that he had to lean against the wall, and flung himself on the bed, soft, warm, comforting after his nights on the summer house floor.

He couldn't get his feet in. He rolled off and switched on the light. He was touched to find that Geoffrey, with all that he had on his mind, had taken the trouble to come upstairs, leaving a trail of wet, black, ashy footprints and make him an apple-pie bed, to make him feel at home.

■ CHAPTER TWENTY-THREE ■

'Why don't you take Bryony with you?' Julian was arrested by his mother's voice as he opened the car door. He opened his mouth to protest, but then said:

'Get in, Bryony.'

'I don't . . .'

'Come on, I haven't got all day.'

Father and daughter slammed themselves into the car. Julian, to show his displeasure, failed to put on his seat belt, as if to say, 'My Saturday morning's been spoiled so I don't care if I get killed.' He valued his Saturday mornings, no one knew where he went; it was his own secret time and now he had an intruder in tow, who was asking:

'Where are we going, Daddy?' and fluttering a hand towards his seat belt. In reply he turned on the radio. The hand withdrew. Bryony realised from the way he swore when they had to stop at a zebra crossing and cursed the red lights and sped away at the amber that they were in a great hurry. They must be going somewhere very important. They were going to see Mummy. She sank back happily in her seat and looked out of the window while a cricket commentary crackled round them from the radio.

Julian found a space in the car park and went to buy a ticket from the machine. When he came back he was extremely irritated to see that she was crying.

'What's the matter now?'

'I didn't bring my card.'

'What card?'

'The card I made for Mummy. The Get Well card.'

'Well, what do you want it now for?'

'To give to Mummy.'

Cars pulled in and reversed. People crossed the car park with loaded trollies as they stared at each other.

'Aren't we going to see Mummy then?' Bryony said at last.

'Don't be so bloody stupid. Why on earth would Mummy be in a Redhill car park?'

'I thought it might be the hospital,' she said in a small voice. As she spoke she knew she hadn't really believed herself that they were going to see Mummy. There flashed into her mind a doll whose legs had come off and which she had stuck back into the sockets at night, hoping that in the morning they would have joined on again. Pink plastic duped hopes fell to the carpet in the curtained light. Julian was pulling her by the arm.

'If you thought this was a hospital you're even stupider than I thought you were. Anyway, Mummy's not in a hospital, she's in a loony bin!' A litter bin loomed as he dragged her along.

'Liar!' muttered Bryony. 'Liar, liar, your pants are on fire!'

'What?'

Nothing. She knew it wasn't true because Nanny had told her Mummy was in hospital for a rest because she wasn't feeling well and would be home in a few days. But Bryony and Nanny could have done all the work. When she got home she would tell Nanny that she could make scrambled egg and tea and toast and Mummy could come home. A loony bin. For the rest of her life whenever she heard these words, a scratched yellow litter bin vomiting battered fish skin and bones would bulge into her thoughts, but now they were entering a D.I.Y. shop. The smell of boredom from the new tiles and chipboards and vinyls assaulted Bryony immediately; she began to yawn. Her father homed in on the bathroom fittings. She trailed after him.

'Don't touch,' he said sharply, although he was doing so. 'Nobody wants to buy things with dirty fingermarks on them.' Then he gave her a little push and said in quite a different voice, 'Go and look at the wallpapers – see if there's anything you'd like for your bedroom. Esther! What brings you here?'

'Oh, I just sometimes come here on a Saturday morning. I love the smell, everything so fresh and new and clean . . .'

'So do I!' he exclaimed delightedly. 'So do I. It's my little relaxation, pottering round, imagining what I could do. There's such potential – ' He broke off.

'Fresh and new and clean,' she had said, standing in a cool checked shirtwaist dress and despite the heat wearing tights; he liked that in a woman.

'Have you got a house, a flat, of your own?'

159

'No. I live with my Aunt and Uncle. I've got my own room, of course, but it's very old-fashioned – I'd love to get my hands on some of those wallpapers.' It was ridiculous; she knew that the world might end on Wednesday and here she was prattling about wallpaper.

'I – I could give you a hand, if you wanted to do any decorating.'

She shook her head. 'I wouldn't be allowed.' Regretfully she dismissed a picture of two people sitting on a step-ladder, paint brushes at rest in their tins, sharing a mug of cocoa.

'You look fresh and clean,' Julian blurted out.

'Pardon? I – listen, there's something I must tell you . . .'

A crash cut across her words. Bryony had brought down a pyramid of paint tins. She had wanted to see if it was true that the whole thing would collapse if you pulled out the bottom ones or if the pile would stand suspended for a moment in air.

Esther ran to pick them up. Julian pulled Bryony roughly by the arm.

'Can't you be trusted for a minute?'

Bryony wouldn't raise her eyes from their feet. Daddy's Nature Treks, which until now she had liked, spread out like broad brown bullies under the ends of his light blue trousers; the lady had flat black round-nosed shoes, and she was wearing those horrible brown tights that Mummy hated.

'Say hello to Miss Beaney.'

A finger was raising her chin so that she was forced to look up. The arm that moved the finger was not the same colour as the legs, being white.

'Hello!'

'Hello, Bryony, and what's your name?'

Bryony stared, she saw that this stupid woman had tied the belt of her dress round her pony tail and one of its ends hung over her shoulder. A slow blush, starting deep below her white plastic belt and creeping under the buttoned neck of her dress, stained Esther's face.

'How silly of me. I mean, how old are you, how are you, I mean!'

'O.K..'

'Well, we must be going. Bryony's Mummy's in hospital,' said Julian over her head.

'Oh dear, poor Daisy. Is it serious?' Julian tapped a finger on his skull. Esther nodded.

'I see. Poor Daisy. I'm not surprised . . . I must go to her.'
Obviously Mummy wouldn't want to see her.
'What about my wallpaper?'
'Never mind that now.'
'Children can be very callous. Julian, I've got to tell you . . .'
But Julian, seeing the manager approaching, was propelling his
daughter out of the shop.
'See you soon, I hope.' He smiled.
When they got to the car park he suddenly pulled her hair, hard.
'That's for being rude to Miss Beaney.'
When she glanced through a glaze at his profile, he was smiling
again.

'What's up with Bryony?' Julian's mother confronted him.
'How should I know?'
'She just dashed past me in tears, saying something about arms
and legs that don't match.'
'She's sulking because I wouldn't buy new wallpaper for her
room.'
'She's missing her Mummy.'
She heard Julian whistling as he went into the garden. His wife
was in hospital, his daughter crying, and he was whistling. She
hadn't understood him for years and she never would. But she did
love him. He was such a lovely baby, such a lovely little boy. She
had tried so hard to make it up to him for not having a father. It was
when he went to the grammar school that he changed. He became
ashamed of her, and their home, and after that it seemed that he
always pushed her away. She had cried herself to sleep more nights
than she could remember.

■ CHAPTER TWENTY-FOUR ■

'You've got a visitor.'

The nurse spoke brightly as if she concealed a lovely present behind the door. Julian's shadow fell across her bed. 'I'll put these in water for you.'

The nurse took a paper sheaf of carnations from Julian and buried her face in them.

'Mmmm, gorgeous! Aren't you the lucky one!' She winked at Daisy as she closed the door.

'My mother bought them. Seventy-five pence! The garden's full of flowers.'

'Why have you come?'

'If you must know I've cancelled an important appointment to come all the way out here to make you face up to your responsibilities. You've got a husband and child and a house to run, remember? Or had you forgotten?'

'No.'

'Look at you lying there! If you could just see yourself! You're not ill. Where are your clothes?'

Daisy's hand reached for the bell; he slapped it down and grabbed a mirror from her locker and thrust it against her face, knotting her hair in his other hand.

'Just look at yourself, look at yourself.'

He banged her forehead against the glass until it broke and a thin stream of blood ran into her eye.

'That's seven years bad luck for you,' she said calmly.

'Seven years bad luck? Seven years! My bad luck started the day I met you. Oh, for God's sake get yourself cleaned up before that nurse comes back.'

He fished a white handkerchief from his pocket, shook it out and then replaced it, pulling a handful of tissues from a box on the locker.

'There are one or two things we've got to get clear. First, who's this soldier you've been carrying on with?'

'Solder?' Soldier. Carrying on with. The red delta on her forehead cut deeper. Her throat dried.

'Don't play the innocent with me.' He bunched the front of her nightdress in his fist, pulling her up.

'Who is he?'

'You're hurting me.'

'I'll hurt you a lot more before I'm through, you dirty little whore. First that teacher and now some soldier. You've never been exactly generous with your favours to me, have you?'

He punctuated his words by banging her head against the iron rails at the bedhead.

'Who is he?'

'Ouch, please, my head—he's—he's my brother.'

'Liar.' He threw her back on the pillow and punched her in the stomach. 'You've got bloody skinny, you know that? Bloody skinny.'

A blow landed on her ribs.

'Sorry I've been so long. They look lovely, don't they?'

The nurse, bearing the carnations in a glass vase, took in the tumbled sheets, the broken smeared glass on the bed.

'Mr Almond, Dr Jones would like a word with you. It's the second door on the left.'

Julian was just not getting through to this Welsh git who faced him across the desk, did not seem to be able to convince him of what he had to put up with. The story of Daisy's elopement and how she had tricked him had failed to impress him. Julian had searched his mind for evidence of her instability, how he had found her on her knees, opening birthday cards for the cat.

'I don't see the problem'—this quack was quacking—'obviously he couldn't open them himself.'

'No, you don't understand; she and the child and the child's friend had made birthday cards for the cat!'

'You mean she'd got the date wrong, it wasn't his birthday?'

'No, it was his birthday,' Julian shouted. 'That's not the point!' He stood up.

'I think, perhaps, that we should consider the possibility that it's you who has the problem. Oh, Mr Almond,' he called, as Julian struggled with the door, 'try turning the handle the other way—I think it would be better if you didn't visit your wife for a while.'

'You're so right.' Julian slammed the door, but it slid silently back on its silver arm. Dr Jones looked up in surprise from his report as it jerked open again.

'You want to know what else she's done? My boss paid her the compliment of inviting her to lunch and she stood him up!'

'There's been a Miss Beaney on the telephone. Three times. She says it's urgent,' his mother told him.

'Did you get her number?'

'She was ringing from a callbox. She said she'd ring back later. Julian, how was Daisy?'

'I do not want to discuss her.'

'Julian,' she attempted to put her arm round his shoulder, 'is there anything I can do to help? I hate to see you unhappy. I am your mother.'

'Unfortunately. Have you been peeling onions? Your hand smells.'

The telephone rang; Julian was gone, leaving his mother's tainted hands empty.

'I'm going to the office, and I'll be out tonight so don't bother to wait up,' he said. 'You can leave me a sandwich if you like. I've got to change this shirt. It smells of hospitals!'

▪ CHAPTER TWENTY-FIVE ▪

'Well, why won't you come into a pub?'

'I can't. I'm not allowed to. It's my religion. And I've got to be specially careful now! I just can't afford to sin.'

A look of desperation crossed her face.

'Well, you won't object if I have some wine with my meal?' he smiled teasingly at her.

She shook her head uncertainly and let herself be led into La Golondrina. She was too distracted to notice the cheerful checked cloths, the candles in their bottles, the wreaths of plastic ivy. Julian watched the soft curves under her blouse as she sat down, but she was twisting her hands together.

'Something terrible's happened – or is going to happen.'

During the past few days she had become increasingly distraught. It was hard to maintain her disbelief in her Uncle's vision. He had made a placard and marched round the streets of Redhill unregarded, expect for an occasional titter, urging people to repent. He had written a letter to *The Times*, but it had not been printed; it was too late to place an ad. in the *Surrey Mirror*. Esther's task was to knock on as many doors as possible so that as many people as possible might be saved. Her feet were blistered; she, red-eyed from worry and lack of sleep, was taking on the aspect of a deranged woman, although she had washed her face and hair before setting out to meet Julian. Her Aunt and Uncle thought that she was canvassing. Her Aunt alternated between flapping to the point of incoherence and sitting smiling calmly with folded hands.

'Of course, you'll be seeing your parents again dear, won't you?' she had remarked, and it was this more than anything that had made Esther wonder if the whole thing might be true and had set her in a panic of fear and anticipation.

She was interrupted by the waiter bringing the food which Julian had ordered.

She wasn't pregnant? As the terrible thought came into Julian's mind it was shamed by the purity of her face. He tasted the wine and spat it back into the glass.

'Cat's pee,' he said, waving the bottle away. He had been impressed once when Giles Cluff-Trench had done the same.

'Sorry,' he said to Esther's affronted face. 'No, you don't tuck your serv – napkin under your chin, you do it like this. Let me.' He leaned across the table and spread the napkin tenderly over her lap, his hand grazing her thighs, but so lightly that she was embarrassed by her blush. Her first time in a proper restaurant, and tomorrow it would all be gone. She shouldn't be here, she should be in the chapel with the rest of them, on her knees, weeping for mercy.

'Esther, you're like a cat on hot bricks! What's wrong? What's the terrible news?'

'Oh, Julian,' she wept, 'the world's going to end at dawn and I may never see you again.'

'What do you mean? Of course the world's not going to end.'

'It is, it is. My Uncle's had a vision.'

Incoherently she told how the Judgement Day was at hand and how only the members of the True Faith would escape the wrath of God. The minibus would leave the chapel at eleven and the congregation would spend the night in a vigil of prayer on Leith Hill, waiting for the dawn.

'Come to the chapel with me Julian, please, please come. It may not be too late for you if you repent now.'

She stood, breast heaving, her pleading hands on his hands.

'But we haven't finished our meal . . .'

'Would you trade a meal for a banquet at God's table?'

'Please Esther, people are looking!'

She slumped back in her chair.

'Why me? Why are you so worried about me?'

She mumbled something to the congealing paella on her plate.

'What did you say?'

'I love you,' she almost shouted and made a bolt for the 'Ladies', but blurred by tears rushed past the little sign and had to withdraw her head quickly from the plastic strips across the entrance to the kitchen, as a startled washer-up turned from the sink and silently pointed a sudsy hand in the right direction.

Carlos sidled up to Julian's table.

'Is everything satisfactory, sir?'

Julian took the rose from the glass on the table and put it in his buttonhole and carefully moved the hands on his watch back one hour.

'Oh yes,' he said, turning on him a smile of such radiance that the worried little man was quite overcome. 'Everything is most satisfactory.'

'Bring me two large gins, in one glass,' he added.

'Sir? You don't like the wine?'

'Just bring it quickly.'

Carlos sighed and shrugged. Julian just had time to pour the gin into Esther's orange juice before she returned, eyes bathed, from the Ladies' Room.

'Feeling better? Drink up your orange.'

She complied meekly.

'Bryony's not very like you, is she?' she said.

'I wouldn't be surprised if she wasn't mine,' he said gloomily.

Their eyes met and dismissed his paternity.

'She's cost me my job now,' said Julian.

'Bryony?'

'Daisy! Apparently, my boss invited her to lunch. She didn't bother to inform me of course. Just stood him up. What do you think of that kind of behaviour, Esther? Surely a man can expect some kind of backing from his wife in his career? Surely he's entitled to that at least?'

'I should jolly well think so! What happened – did he sack you?'

'Of course not.' Julian rejected the suggestion contemptuously. 'He came back to the office in a foul mood. He'd been waiting for over an hour. No doubt she had a pressing engagement with a soldier – no, I haven't found out anything definite – she's such a liar. Tried to say it was her brother! Anyway, the upshot was we had words and it ended with me telling him to stuff his job.'

'Good for you!'

'Yes, but don't you see, my career! All those years down the drain, just when I was getting somewhere—'

'Oh, Julian, how awful, you poor thing.' She took his hand and he remembered her kindness in the chemist's.

'And then that bloody psychiatrist has the nerve to tell me that it's me who's round the bend!'

'These trick cyclists are all the same,' comforted Esther with the confidence of one who had never met one.

'What the hell am I going to do?'

His words reminded her of her mission.

'What's the time, Julian? We should be going.' She started to fumble for her handbag and dropped it.

'Relax. It's only half-past eight. Don't worry, we'll get to the chapel in plenty of time.'

'Oh, good. Funny, I would've thought it was much later. I'm awfully thirsty, Julian. Could I have another orange, please?'

'Same again for the lady,' Julian winked at Carlos.

'Oh, I do like the way you talk to the waiters, so masterful,' sighed Esther. 'I can see they respect you.'

'I am not the waiter. It is the waiter's night off,' said Carlos, but no one heard him.

'I think I must have done something very wicked in a former life that I should serve people like these and always smiling, smiling,' he told Stanley in the kitchen gloomily, pouring himself a glass of wine, 'only I don't remember what it was. I just hope I enjoyed it. That man's a fool, he knows nothing about wine.'

'Oh dear, I promised Aunt Hannah I'd give her a hand with the sandwiches! Please, Julian, can't we go now?'

'Sandwiches?'

'For the vigil. She's doing the refreshments. Uncle Amos was furious. He said we ought to fast, but she said she'd already bought the ham and it was a shame to waste good food. He said he wasn't going to kneel before the Throne with a ham sandwich in his mouth. She made herself a new skirt too, he was cross about that as well, but she said, "It's not every day you go to meet your Maker . . ." Oh, dear, we'd better hurry, I'm sure it's late, and it's raining again . . .'

Julian checked the bill and could not fault it. They were the only customers left.

'I'm not going to leave a tip because the wine was too warm,' Julian explained courteously as he pocketed his change. 'Keeps them on their toes,' he said to Esther. 'They'll make an extra effort next time.'

'There ain't gonna be no next time,' muttered Carlos under his smile but Esther heard. Stanley had come out with a plastic can and was watering the plants in the window. Carlos's words were like a shaft of light in her clouded brain, illuminating the chapel and Leith Hill.

'I wouldn't bother to do that if I was you,' she said thickly, waving a vague arm. Julian caught it and guided her through the door.

'I think I feel a bit funny.'

'It was too hot in there. Come along, the car's just across the road.'

In the car her head dropped onto his shoulder.

'I'm so happy that you're coming with me. We'll be together through all eternity – to think I might never have met you.' She shuddered. 'We won't be late, will we? Julian!' She sat up straight suddenly. 'You do love me too, don't you? Only, I don't think you said . . .' Her voice trailed off.

'I love you,' said Julian.

'That's all right then.' She snuggled down sleepily. 'It was love at first sight for me, was it for you?'

'Mmmm.'

'Then it was love at first sight for both of us. It's good really, isn't it – the world ending now? I mean, you being saved just in time, there won't be any problem about you being married, will there? I mean, Daisy . . .'

A little doubt wormed its way through the wine and started wriggling. What if the old loony was right? The windscreen blurred with sudden rain and a dark blob of blood, like a cracked mirror. He put on the wipers but the dead insect was just outside their arc and he had to drive on with it hanging there until a heavy gust of rain, in a burst of thunder, washed it off. He wished he had not given Esther that gin; he ground his teeth at her innocently slurred speech. He had feared that the evening would end with a chaste goodnight outside her crazy chapel, for he had no intention of entering it, unless he did something to prevent it, and now perhaps he had placed her soul in jeopardy. Of course it was all nonsense, but . . .

'Oh, it's so dark. I'm scared. Did you see that lightning? Pray, please pray! Will it always be dark, do you think?' She gripped his hand on the wheel and started to mutter frantically.

'Where the hell is this chapel?'

She peered through the steamy window, wiping futilely at the inside of the wet pane.

'I don't know where we are. We should have been here by now. We must have gone past.'

'Oh God!'

'No, hang on. Try the next left. Dear God, in your infinite mercy . . .'

A savage fork of lightning ripped the black sky and the car was forced to the side of the road by a fire engine and then an ambulance, see-sawing sirens shrieking louder than the thunder. Esther screamed. 'There. It's up there! Oh God, don't let us be too late! I hope the minibus hasn't left.'

As Esther almost fell from the car, Julian pulled her back. Firemen were directing a jet of water at the black shell which was all that was left of the True Faith Chapel. Clouds of steam hissed as the water hit the burning tin. Walkie-talkies crackled; a policeman held back the little crowd; a procession of stretchers was being carried to the ambulances.

Esther ran to claw at a red blanket and a policeman restrained her in the blue revolving lights of the ambulances and fire engines and police cars. To whom could she turn but Julian? He held her hand throughout the making of statements to the police, the identification of the victims. It was hard to believe in the resurrection of the body when confronting the corpses of Aunt Hannah and Uncle Amos.

'It seems as though the door jammed,' a fireman told them. 'They didn't stand a chance once the roof collapsed. Some sort of church, wasn't it? I don't suppose you'll be able to claim anything on the insurance. What they call an Act of God.'

'I'll take you home,' Julian said.

Esther fitted her key into the lock. Her hand shook.

'I don't want to go in.'

'Here, let me.' He turned the key and pushed her gently through the door into darkness. He fumbled for a light switch. They stood blinking in the tiny hall under the garish bulb in its old cracked shade in the storm of ancient oak leaves papering the walls.

'Where's the kitchen? I'll make some tea.'

In the midst of her tears the thought passed through Esther's mind that she was as good as Daisy now, here was a man making tea for her; better, because he was Daisy's husband. Then she was recalled to her genuine grief by her aunt's apron on a hook.

'I should have been there.'

Julian stirred his tea, the spoon clashed against the sides of his cup, slopping tea onto the table. His forehead was creased with thought. He cleared his throat, the words came thickly.

'It must have been meant. God's will, I mean, ahem.' He cleared his throat again. 'He must have wanted you to live.'

Esther, unaware of any embarrassment or insincerity or his difficulty in pronouncing the name of God except in profanity, looked up at him through swollen eyes.

'Yes, you must be right. Thank you, Julian. I don't know what I'd have done without you.'

She started to cry again.

'I'd always like to be here when you need me,' he said. 'Drink your tea.'

'You're so good.' She obeyed him.

'I'm not really, you know.' He took her hands. He wanted to lay his head in her lap and confess to the gin, to hitting Daisy in hospital, about his mother and Bryony. 'I'm not good. I haven't been a good son or husband or father.' As he said it, he felt something like a boil burst inside him and the bitterness dissolve. He thought that he would never hit anyone again. The tea flowed through him like an antidote to years of poison. Sitting in the little kitchen somewhere between night and morning, the rain sluicing down outside, at the bare table between the stone sink and the old grey mottled cooker, he felt peace wash over him.

'Julian?'

'Yes.'

'Don't go, please. Please stay. I don't want to be alone.'

'Of course I'll stay.'

'I don't know where you can sleep. I suppose we could push two chairs together.' They both knew that he could not sleep in the dead people's bed.

'Let me just lie beside you, in your bed. Then I'll be there if you need me. I won't do anything, I promise.'

'Thank you. Shall we go up then?'

As they passed her Aunt and Uncle's room, Esther staggered against him. He held her and she cried in his arms.

'My sweet, my love, my angel,' he babbled, stroking her hair, then her neck, her shoulder. 'Don't cry, my darling, don't cry,' he groaned and then his hand somehow slipped between the buttons of her blouse and found her breast and then her body with a last long shuddering sob was against his and her mouth all wet with tears was on his mouth. As they entered the bedroom, all entwined, he slipped a wooden cross from a nail on the wall and dropped it behind the dressing table. At the bed, Esther drew back.

'Don't, please, don't.'

171

'I'm sorry.' He kissed the top of her head.

Esther woke suddenly and sat upright.

'I keep thinking it's all a bad dream, but it isn't, is it? It's true. What's the time?' She went over to the window. 'Look!'

Vast voluptuous baroque pearls tumbled about the sky, great pink-tinged shells, and through them streamed the sun in long straight golden rods, pouring radiance onto the earth.

'Everything's all right,' she whispered. 'They're happy, I know it.'

Gold pools glittered in every wet cabbage leaf, the roses sparkled, a row of diamonds on the clothes line shot brilliants everywhere, a benign steam rose gently from the path and fence as blue soaked slowly through the sky. They stood side by side listening to the bird song.

'Will you be able to stay on here for a while?' he murmured into her hair, released from its band, fanned about her back.

'The house is mine now.'

'Yours?'

'Uncle Amos left it to me. He told me.'

'It could be quite a bijou residence.' Julian tried to keep the excitement out of his voice. Esther laid her arms against the window, her breath clouding the glass, smearing it with tears.

'You'll get cold standing there. A woman of property, eh?'

He carried her back to bed.

▪ CHAPTER TWENTY-SIX ▪

Daisy looked down at her legs, mummified in the white sheet. She had to acknowledge reluctantly that her metamorphosis was over, that her sojourn in the vegetable kingdom had been brief. She tried, but could not will her feet back into roots. Still, no one else need know yet that she was flesh again. It was pleasant in the little room, although she knew she would not be permitted to remain there much longer. There had been already threats of the Ward, exhortations to get up. Her eyes swam in weak tears. Suddenly the word 'Oberammergau' floated in front of her and in the instant, as it did, she wondered if Esther's story had been true. There was only an Oberammergau Passion Play every ten years or so; surely she had read something about one being staged next year, some protest about men playing all the parts? But why should Esther make it up? Was Esther Beaney, in fact, mad?

Two flies buzzed under the lampshade, Stanley's manuscript and Seamus; and were joined by her failure of Seamus, her mother-in-law, Jennifer Greengrass, Esther Beaney, Uncle Stanley. She closed her eyes but they circled on, round and round, round and round, droning louder and louder, until she buried her head in the pillow, but could not drown; then Finchy stood in the centre of the room, huge, growing towards the ceiling; suddenly her tongue uncurled in a sticky roll of flypaper . . .

'You've been dreaming . . .'

'Uncle Stanley!'

Stanley stood beside her bed with a brown paper bag in his hand.

'I thought you might like some grapes.'

He put the bag on the table that straddled the end of her bed. He seemed to have shrunk since last she saw him. His wrists poked out of the skimpy sleeves of his jacket, she looked at them: bone blades fuzzed with gold, vulnerable and growing old, and felt hot tears well up in her eyes and gush out. Once started, she couldn't stop.

'Don't, don't – have a grape.'

Stanley grazed a cold grape against her lip. It burst its black skin on her teeth, spilling its green flesh and pips, making her laugh and choke and cry the more.

'What is it, tell me?' He patted her leg through its thick padding, awkwardly.

'Everything,' she sobbed, in such a childish desolate way that his glasses misted up. He put his arm round her shoulder and pulled her to him. She wept on his chest, the rough kindly tweed, the soft shirt, and at last looked up to see his glasses clouded with compassion. He stroked her head.

'Your shirt. I'm sorry.'

'It doesn't matter.'

He wound her hair round his finger.

'Is there anything I can do?'

'There's nothing anyone can do.'

'Is it Julian?'

She shook her head.

'What then?'

'It's too late, too late. Nobody can do anything.'

'It may not be too late . . .'

'She's dead, isn't she? How can that not be too late? And I killed her.'

'Who's dead?'

He pulled out his handkerchief and pressed it into her hand and then directed her hand to her face.

'Jennifer Greengrass.' She could hardly get the name out. It was the first time she had spoken it aloud and it floated like a coffin on the air.

'What do you mean – you killed her?'

'You must know. Everybody knows. She took an overdose because of me. Her children, oh – when I think of Bryony—'

She flung herself face downwards on the pillow. When she raised her head Stanley had gone. No wonder he could not bear to be with her, when she could not bear to be with herself. Then the door opened and a telephone on a trolley bumped through, followed by Stanley with a directory.

He plugged the telephone in beside her bed. She raised herself on one elbow.

'What are you doing?' she asked fearfully.

He didn't answer but sat down on the bed and opened the

directory, turned the pages and then started running a finger down the list of names. His finger stopped. He took Daisy's finger and placed it beside his.

She looked.

Greengrass, T.

'No, no, I won't speak to him. I can't!' She tried to pull her hand away.

'Dial the number.'

'No, no. I can't.' She managed to jerk her hand from his.

'All right then, I will.'

He did. Shaking, she heard it ring. As the ringing stopped, Stanley forced the receiver into her hand and jammed it against her ear.

'44774' said a woman's voice. 'Hullo, 44774,' it repeated a little impatiently. 'Jennifer Greengrass speaking . . .'

The receiver fell to the bed. Stanley replaced it.

'But, but . . . I thought . . .'

'Why did you think she was dead?'

'But she must be! Finchy said . . '

'Ah, Finchy!'

Some time later Daisy got up to wash her face. The words 'a handful of aspirins – discharged the next day' blazed in the air about her like golden garlands brushing against her as she went into the bathroom. The water broke in a million diamonds on the basin and washed away the black years one by one, like layers of grime. As she looked round for a towel her eye fell on a bathroom scale on the floor. Bloody skinny he had said. Bloody skinny. She stepped onto the scales, her feet stood below the glass bubble where the needle trembled, flesh, not root; wonderful bone. She looked down at the needle. She jumped off the scales and shrieked, 'I've lost half a stone!' and ran out into the room, her face still dripping, where Dr Jones stood with Stanley.

'Stanley, Doctor, I've lost half a stone! Where are my clothes? I've got to go home – I'm better – I'm not ill – I've got to see my daughter – Oh! where are my shoes?'

'Dr Jones said I can take you home. I'll call a taxi while you dress.'

'Keep away from the phosphates!' Dr Jones called after them as they left.

*　　*　　*

'He's gone, Daisy – he's gone! He came and took all his clothes in a suitcase. He said he wasn't coming back. I'm sorry, love.' Julian's mother burst into tears. 'Not a very happy homecoming.'

Daisy ran through the house, switching on all the lights, turning the taps on full blast, the radio; flooding the house and garden with music as she ran out, drunk on air, on grass, on light, the flowers, battered but radiant after last night's storm. Then she saw the tortoise, Mark, quietly cropping clover. She picked him up; the earth swung under his shell, the sky arched blue; water and sun and music blazed in glory.

In the taxi, on the way home to Hope Villa, Stanley put his hand to his shirt, now dry. It was a long time since a woman had been in his arms. He must remedy it.

■ CHAPTER TWENTY-SEVEN ■

'Come on, Jason, we've got to get this place cleaned up.'

'Why?'

'Because we've got people coming to tea.'

Coming to tea was a new concept for Jason. 'Why?'

'Because my niece and her little girl are coming to see me. Us.'

'What's a niece?'

'She's my brother's daughter. I'm her uncle.'

Jason did not look pleased. 'I don't want you to be her uncle.'

'I'm still your uncle, you silly boy. Now tell me, do you think a vase, a jam-jar of flowers would look nice on the table, or do you think it would just point up the general squalor, the meanness of the aspect, mmm? Shall we buy some flowers?'

'No.'

'Yes, I think we will. Now if you'll just sit on the bed while I sweep the floor . . .' Stanley, intent on his dusting, suddenly realised that Jason was very quiet. He turned round; Jason was standing on a chair at the basin, busy with the soap and a nailbrush.

'What are you doing?'

'I'm cleanin' the sink for you.'

The new soap was dirty and printed with black crescents, scored by the nailbrush whose bristles were splayed.

'Good boy,' said Stanley. 'I'll just wash the soap and then we can go. Now what shall we buy for tea?'

'Chips.'

'No, I don't think chips. Cakes and things. Perhaps some salad, lemonade . . .'

'Can we have salad cream?'

'Of course we can. I'd say it was essential, wouldn't you?'

'And ice cream?'

'Certainly, but we'll have to ask Nanny if we can put it in her fridge.'

'She's gone out.'

'Of course she has. No problem then. Come on, Jase.'

Before going into Waitrose, Stanley took Jason into Websters. He thought it was time he had some books of his own. Jason sat on the floor surrounded by brightly coloured piles of books, pulling more and more from the shelf, to the disapproval of the assistants, who were on the point of intervening, trying to decide between two animal picture books.

'I like animals,' said Jason.

Stanley bought them both. He did not let himself think about the hole this shopping spree was going to make in his shallow pocket. Jason sat on the low shelf under Waitrose's window with a book in one hand, the other upending a tube of Smarties into his mouth.

Out they came, crossed the road, waiting to let a truck of cattle turn into the abbatoir, and then had to cross again further down at the lights to go to the tobacconist's for cigarettes and an ice lolly.

The pavement was crowded with mid-morning shoppers. A woman bumped into Jason, knocking his lolly from his hand.

'Cow,' he said.

Stanley blushed. 'I do apologise . . .' he began, but 'Cow,' said Jason again loudly.

'Well really, some people aren't fit to . . .' She stopped open-mouthed.

A mad heifer was bolting through the traffic. Cars swerved and screeched and hooted; someone screamed, two men with sticks, one in bloody white overalls, came pounding down the pavement, scattering shoppers.

'Head it off!'

The traffic in both directions came to a halt, a cacophony of horns came from those behind, unable to see the cause of the snarl-up. People ran from shops to see, trapped drivers trembled for their paintwork. The beast turned at bay between two lorries.

'Are they going to shoot it?' asked Jason and at the same time Stanley stuck his foot out instinctively and sent the slaughterman thudding to the pavement with his stick twisting painfully through his legs. The heifer leaped sideways and veered onto the pavement. People pressed themselves back against the shop windows. It seemed to gather itself up on its hind legs to leap, but there was nowhere to go, and for a second the animal's eyes held Stanley's and sent an agonised plea boring into them and then rolled upwards into white blanks as the irises disappeared and the heifer reared and jumped backwards.

'Nice cow!'

'Jason!'

But Jason put out a hand to grab its tail as it turned and slipped out of the other pursuer's hand. He was pulled screaming into the road just as an impatient lorry driver put his foot down. Stanley hurtled forward and knocked him out of the way and received the full impact of a front wheel.

He was carried into Culpeper, the Herbalists, and as he was laid on the floor his foot caught the corner of a big wicker basket and scented cushions and herb pillows fell about him. Old rose petals, distilled summers, his mother's dresses; the Dreamland Express came hurtling down the line. Someone had put his shopping bag beside him; his hand fluttered towards it. It sagged and a yellow bottle rolled away. The girl from Culpeper's bent to hear, above the siren of the ambulance, the hoarse words he was whispering:

'Salad cream.'

'What did he say?'

'"It's all a dream." He said, "It's all a dream."'

She began to cry.

The herbal remedies in the cellophane packets in the drawers, the perfumed pyramids of soap; the stretcher with its red blanket. Two wasps stopped attacking a honeycomb on the dresser and circled above a pool on the floor. Stanley was carried out to the ambulance where Jason sat, the tracks of tears on his dirty face hidden by the peak of the driver's cap.

■ CHAPTER TWENTY-EIGHT ■

The spoiled pillows had been written off on the appropriate form and consigned to the stockroom; the floor had been scrubbed; parts of the heifer no doubt hung in the butcher's window. The *Dorking Advertiser* carried the headline: 'Local Author's Brother Dies Saving Child' above a photograph of Rex holding Jason.

Mrs Finch, coming out of Woolworth's, was struck by a poster on the news-stand: 'Hero Saves Child: Dies.'

She had been glad to get out of the house this morning; it was like a morgue with Lady Muck lying in bed all day and him, shut in his study in a cloud of smoke, emerging only in the evening to grope his way, red-eyed, to the cellar. And guess who had to take out the empties. The nice bit of beef she had got them had shrivelled in its gravy and grown cold. She had had to eat it herself to save waste and had shared the left-overs, in sandwiches, with a reporter from London. They had refused to see him. She bought an early edition of the *Evening Standard* and stood in the street greedily sucking in its print. There was no article. No mention of the motherly house-keeper keeping the sinking ship afloat single-handed. When he had asked her name she had to think for a moment – it was so long since anyone had used it. 'Theda,' she said at last. 'That's it – Theda. Like the film star.' She screwed the paper up and thrust it into the litter bin. Lot of fuss about nothing. They never even liked him!

She crossed the road and headed for Quality Seconds. She was in quest of something to wear for the funeral. When she had gone to her ladyship's room that morning to explain that she had nothing suitable, a hand had groped out of the tumbled bedclothes, fumbled at the bedside table for a handbag and flung it at her. As Finchy scrabbled among its spilled contents on the floor, her eye was caught by an old creased letter that bore the signature 'Stanley' in faded ink. 'He wouldn't be writing you love-letters if he could see you now,' she muttered, as she pocketed the ten pounds which was all there was in the purse.

Mrs Finch pushed her way through the heavy doors of Quality Seconds. Something black was what she was after. She curled her lip at the circular rack of gaudy cotton skirts.

'This is all you can offer?' she demanded. 'Not much of a selection, is it?'

She was directed to a group of crimplene skirts, suspended from hangers on the wall. She raked through them until she found a black, waist 32 inches. She pulled it down and marched over to the door to examine it in the light for flaws but could find nothing wrong except the poor finishing-off inside.

'Bit shoddy, isn't it? Look at this seam! Sweated labour, I suppose.' She sniffed. 'Well, I suppose I'll have to try it on, if that's the best you can do.'

As she disappeared into the changing room she heard a voice through the curtain:

'Well, what d'you expect for £3.99?'

And was aware of an invisible tongue thrust at her back. In reality Mrs Finch was well pleased. She slipped off her own skirt and zipped up the other; it would do very well.

'Oh, I didn't realise there was anyone in here . . .' A woman of about her own age stood, with a black shiny blouse over her arm.

'Just a minute, let's have a look at that blouse?'

'Pardon?'

'Let me have a look at that blouse. It's just what I'm looking for.'

'I was just going to try it on.'

'They got any more like that?'

'No, they haven't and this one's mine!'

'What size is it? Let's have a look.'

'Get your hands off it. Who do you think you are?'

'Haven't paid for it yet, have you? So I'm as much entitled to it as what you are.'

She tore it from behind the other's back, where she was holding it protectively.

'Size 18. You'd never get into that!'

'Give it back! Miss, Miss,' she called plaintively. 'I'm being assaulted.'

'Ladies, please . . .'

The other woman snatched back the blouse with a ripping sound. Finchy slapped her hard across the face. A gust of powder and gin vapour came from her mouth like the spore of a burst puffball.

'Don't you hit my Nan.'

A bullet burst from the little group which had gathered in the doorway and bashed its head into Finchy's stomach, battering her with its fists, and bounced back. Finchy sagged forward, winded, and as she gasped and clutched herself, a nightdress dislodged itself in the attack, slipped slowly down under her skirt, until it reached the ground.

'My lip's bleedin'.'

'He's cut his lip, poor little thing. It's a disgrace.'

The two gladiators heaved and glared.

'It so happens,' panted Finchy, 'I need that blouse for a funeral.'

'So do I,' wheezed her opponent.

'Liar!'

'I'm going to send for the police,' said the shop assistant, turning to go.

'Let her have the bloody blouse. I wouldn't touch it now.'

Shaking, she picked up her shopping bag and stalked off, followed by her little protector who had stemmed his cries with a Malteser from a bag handed to him by a sympathetic lady. His nanny jerked him by the arm.

'Come on, you!'

The sweets flew from his hand and rolled about the floor; the woman and wailing child crunched their way out, leaving the triumphant Finchy to gird up her nightdress and pay for her spoils.

'You ought to knock something off that blouse – it's ripped under the arm.'

The assistant was too afraid to disagree.

■ CHAPTER TWENTY-NINE ■

The sun that shone on the mourners picked out the white chalk on Box Hill above the cemetery and made the gravestones glitter, gave a slick shine and gloss to the leaves and petals of the heaped wreaths, for those whose eyes were in a state to observe. Rex was there and Daphne in a hat with a spotted veil, Mrs Finch beside them, granite in her black, Mrs Herring on the other side of the grave, holding Jason – dressed like a little man in a brown three-piece-suit with a tartan tie on elastic round the neck – firmly by the wrist; Jason's mother, making a rare appearance, her tragic expression perhaps due to the fact that the gravel path had stripped the leather from the backs of her high slender heels. Carlos from La Golondrina sobbing so openly from time to time during the ceremony he had to wring out his moustache and was not quelled even when Daphne lifted her veil at him, a sombre young waiter; Maud, who had braved Daphne and dared to stand, her cleavage bared to the sun, in a black cotton dress, a black handkerchief at her eye, on the arm of a giant who threatened to burst out of an ancient pin-striped suit and who played nervously with his black bow tie throughout the ceremony, as if he expected that at any time it might leap forward and spin into a whirligig of coloured sparks. Beside him was Seamus in jeans, a black T-shirt and leather jacket, his tribute to the solemnity of the occasion; he had won his battle with his mother who had deemed it fitter that he should wear the uniform of his former school. So that is Seamus; what a little thug he looks, Daphne thought, and at that moment he raised his eyes, tears had turned them turquoise and pink and Daphne, un-accountably ashamed, dropped her eyes. The lady from the news-agent's was there and several people whom nobody knew, acquaintances, or the curious drawn by the poignancy of the tale, and a reporter and photographer from the local paper; and alone, slightly apart, Daisy. 'I wish Stanley was here, then I could stand with him,' she thought, and then realised.

Mrs Herring lifted her eyes from the open grave and there was that woman, in her blouse. Her face smarted in memory. She nudged her daughter, who withdrew her arm.

'That's her. That woman I was telling you about. The nerve! Standing there as if butter wouldn't . . .'

At that moment, Mrs Finch had to raise her arm to swipe at a bee or wasp which had alighted on her hair.

'Ha! Pity she couldn't get any black cotton to mend that blouse. That red really shows up in the sunlight!'

'Shut up, Mother. Show a bit of respect,' hissed her daughter.

'Man that is born of woman has but a short time to live and is full of misery. He . . .'

'Where's Uncle Stanley?' pierced the vicar's words. People dropped their eyes or glanced at the coffin and away again quickly. His Nan dredged up something from the dark floor of her mind.

'He's gone to see Baby Jesus.'

Jason pulled at the elastic of his tie and let it ping back on his shirt.

'. . . cut down like a flower . . .' The vicar's voice was drowned by an aggrieved wail.

'I want to see Baby Jesus! I want to go to see Baby Jesus. I want to —' which could not be silenced until Carlos stepped forward and placed a menthol cough sweet in the open mouth. Jason gulped, then coughed, then choked and then deposited the offending sweet in a heap of half-digested chips at the graveside.

Through the heavy coffin-lid, Rex fancied he saw, in a fleeting moment, Stanley's embalmed lips draw back in the ghost of a smile.

Time had become an enemy, octopus-like, which no matter how many times it was stabbed, curled out yet another tentacle to suck him into a sea of nothingness. He had tried to drown it with drink, but that only made it tighten its grip and clench his heart more acutely; its grey arm pulled him back, as if he was an exhausted swimmer who had almost gained the shore of an island, from sleep into its own grey bitter sea where he must toss all night while regrets, lost chances, hopes of redemption bobbed past like spars of wreckage and were carried just out of reach of his grasping fingers into the past.

Rex was borne on its current into Dorking, where he drifted about the streets and was washed up for a moment outside the window of a junk shop. A notice caught his eyes. 'Want to get rid of Auntie's Old Junk? Grandma's Grotties? Whole Houses Cleared. Deceased Effects removed at Good Prices.'

He knew that he must go to Stanley's room. Daphne had told him so several times and Mrs Herring had been on the telephone about it. Daphne had threatened to go herself but he could not bear the thought of Stanley's life exposed to her like a virus culture on a microscope's slide. The callous little notice told him that now was the time to go.

Jason was trundling up and down the path on a plastic bus with an ambulance driver's cap on his head. 'Uncle Stanley's dead,' he informed Rex's back conversationally. 'I found a dead mouse in the garden and I picked it up with my spoon. It didn't have no head. I throwed it in the dustbin.'

'Why is he wearing that cap?' Rex asked Mrs Herring hoarsely when she opened the door.

'He won't be parted from it. He even wears it in bed, don't you, Jase?'

'I won't be parted from it!' said Jason in a knowing way, clasping his hands on his head as if he though Rex might try.

'No worst, there is none . . .' said Rex to himself as he stood once more in his brother's room. He sat down heavily in the greasy chair. The dead clothes hung on the back of the door. The air was sour. It seemed to him as he sat with his face in his hands that all Stanley's sighs and bitter exhalations swarmed like motes of dust through his fingers and into his lungs.

'Wotcher doin'?'

He had heard, dully, a bumping on the stairs and now a red bus was driven into the room.

Rex pulled out the box of books; he pulled the suitcases from under the bed. He would have to bring the car round. But the clothes still hung, the socks trembled on a string above the sink, the empty plimsolls lolled. Something green glittered. A cheap glass jug, holding a thick cracked yellow crust that had been milk, wore a lace cap fringed with green glass beads. Rex crunched them in his hand. Those beads; his grandmother's table; the green and white cloth, the heavy silver knives and forks, the green and gold latticed plates, the tall green glasses for the twins' milk, the Lea and Perrins in its silver castle. Castles on the beach; Stanley had built one called Pearly Towers, decked with razor shells and mussels and shards of mother-of-pearl. His own fort was a poor creation beside it. Rex had kicked down Pearly Towers just as Father and Mother had strolled onto the beach.

'Rex has made a splendid castle, with a moat!' Mother had cried and Father had given him sixpence. Stanley was smacked for being a jealous cry-baby.

Rex ran a finger over the keys of Stanley's old black typewriter.

'Wotcher doin'? Are you writin' with Uncle Stanley's typewriter? I can write with it, shall I show you?'

Rex clasped the machine in both hands as if he would lift it and crash it down on something, but instead he said:

'Yes, show me. Which is "S" for Stanley?' and his head fell forward onto the keys and he cradled the typewriter in his arms, and wept.

▪ CHAPTER THIRTY ▪

'Finchy, Finchy,' Daphne's voice trailed like a weak bird through the house. She had colonised Rex's side of the bed and lay back on four pillows.

'Pass me my engagement diary? . . . Oh Lord, I knew it – I've got to judge a competition at Pebblecombe W.I. Oh God, why can't everybody leave me alone? "An arrangement of wild flowers in an eggcup" – Oh God.' Her face brightened. 'Finchy, you don't suppose you – no' and fell again, as she assessed her. 'No, I can't disappoint them. I'll just have to go. Give me my dressing gown, and run a bath for me, would you?'

Half an hour later Mrs Finch looked disapprovingly at Daphne's legs; indecently smooth, too slim, too girlish, the legs that time forgot, where were the veins and lumps that were rightly hers? She ought to be in prescription support hose by now and, to cap it all, her toenails were painted scarlet.

'Isn't there enough suffering in this world without people arranging flowers in egg cups?' she asked piteously. 'Isn't there anything to eat? I haven't had my lunch.'

'You said you couldn't face anything,' Finchy reminded her.

'I'll be ill if I don't eat. Not that you'd care – not that anyone would care. No one will ever know how Stanley's death has affected me. Finchy, I'm growing old, old and lonely – what's this?'

She poked at a pan in the sink.

'It's only the saucepan I heated up a bit of soup in for my dinner.'

'Really Finchy, it's too bad! It's not fair. There am I lying upstairs on my bed of grief, starving to death, and you are living off the fat of the land down here.'

Finchy was standing four square in front of the cupboard that housed the pedal bin. Daphne pushed her aside and, wrenching open the cupboard, scrabbled about in the bin.

'Aha!' she cried triumphantly on her knees, waving a tin in the air. 'Found you out! Game soup! Was there no tomato or mushroom soup that you must indulge yourself on 85 pence worth of venison while I lie on my sick-bed?'

'I fancied something tasty,' said Finchy, unrepentantly. 'I've had a nasty taste in my mouth all the morning, just like fried—'

'That's enough, Finchy.' Daphne guarded her ears with her hands. 'I don't think in my present state of health I could bear to contemplate the interior of your mouth.'

Nevertheless, ten minutes later they were seated opposite each other at the kitchen table, sharing a plate of pressed tongue sandwiches, like old friends.

As she drove back from Pebblecombe, the prizewinning flowers drooping at her lapel, the tea and cakes she had consumed lay heavily upon Daphne, the sweet crumbs turning to the taste of melancholy. She fought, and succumbed to the impulse to visit the place of Stanley's death. Potpourri and stephanotis filled the air.

'Did he, do you know, say anything before he died? Somebody's name perhaps?'

'He said, "It's all a dream." Those were his last words.'

'It's all a dream,' said Daphne to herself. 'It's all a dream,' as she entered Rex's study, and found him at bay, attacked by Daisy and Seamus. It was she who had formed the plan to save Rex's face and to which they, reluctantly in Seamus's case, at last agreed.

Rex said, to the red condemning head and the brown accusing him: 'For years I thought it was guilt that stopped me from writing my masterwork, although I hadn't the courage to rid myself of the burden. I always set my work against *Silence* and it never measured up to it. I used to think that if I confessed to what I'd done I would be purged and then be able to become the great writer I thought I was, but I couldn't face the disgrace, you see. I did try to burn the manuscript once, but I had to pull it from the flames. Now I know that I have been the artist I am capable of being, and in a strange way I am at peace with myself at last. Besides, you will be pleased to know that last thing of Stanley's is far, far better than anything I could ever write. He should enjoy quite a posthumous success.'

'Stanley has redeemed us and now he's gone,' said Daisy quietly. 'It's too late!'

'It's better than nothing, isn't it?' he almost pleaded.

'I don't know.'

'Your father is already engaged on sorting out Stanley's writing and will have it published as soon as possible. I myself shall write a memoir telling the truth about the authorship of *Silence*. I shall say that it was a literary hoax, a prank. People expect such things of twins. But now that Stanley is dead Rex wants the world to know the truth. I shall call my memoirs *It's All a Dream*.'

'Have you decided what you're going to do yet, Daisy?' Rex played with a paper-weight, not looking at his daughter.

'Not yet. We can't stay at Fairlawn, of course. It's got to be sold. I'm looking for a job. Of course, I'm rather limited by the fact that I can't do anything . . . Why did you let me believe Jennifer Greengrass was dead?' she said suddenly. 'Why did you do nothing to help me, all those years?'

'Don't upset your father any more now,' said Daphne. 'He's had enough.'

Daisy and Seamus walked out of St Cloud.

Rex's head was bent over a pile of papers on his desk; the lamp, for the afternoons grew gloomy early now, shone on a few silver threads in his gold hair. A pair of spectacles slipped down his nose and he pushed them up on his forehead and ground a fist in his eye as if to shift an unpleasant image, the sight he had never thought to see: his two children, together in this room accusing him. He shivered; now there always seemed to be a cold empty space at his side.

Daphne came into the room.

'Won't you stop for today?'

He shook his head.

'I do wish we could work together at the long table as we used. I've finished my children's stories . . . What about old Max? You said you had an idea for him?'

He shook his head again. Behind her through the window, rooks flapped into a black tree like summer betrayals homing through the falling leaves to huddle in his branches.

'Read this.'

He handed her a letter. Daphne looked at the blue straggly words striding the page of cheap writing paper . . .

Hope Villa
Dorking.

Dear Rex,

Mrs Herring told me that you called – I'm sorry I missed you. I think I may know why you came to see me and if I'm right I want you to know that that matter means nothing to me; it's far too long ago to be of any importance and nothing would be gained from raking up the past. After all, what does it matter which twin did what? I do hope that we can meet soon; I look forward very much to seeing you.

Your loving brother,
Stanley.

Daphne handed the letter back.

'Well, that's all right then,' she said.

'Why did he have to behave so well?' Rex burst out, banging his head on the desk. 'He's won.'